Jacques Bellange

*c.*1575–1616

Printmaker of Lorraine

Bellange fecit

Jacques Bellange

*c.*1575–1616

Printmaker of Lorraine

Antony Griffiths and
Craig Hartley

Published for the British Museum
by British Museum Press

© 1997 The Trustees of the British Museum

Published by British Museum Press
A division of The British Museum Company Ltd
46 Bloomsbury Street, London WC1B 3QQ

A catalogue record for this book is available from
the British Library

ISBN 0-7141-2611-X

Edited by Colin Grant

Designed and formatted by James Shurmer

Printed in Great Britain by BAS Printers Ltd

FRONTISPIECE *The Adoration of the Magi* (no. 10)

Contents

Preface

During the first decades of the seventeenth century an extraordinarily wide range of styles and manners of composition flourished simultaneously in European art. In Italy it was the period when the very different revolutions of the Carracci family and Caravaggio set themselves against the still vigorous late Mannerism of Cavaliere d'Arpino and others. In Flanders they were the years when Rubens struck out in a new direction. In the breakaway United Provinces it was, as a recent exhibition termed it, 'the dawn of the Golden Age': the future belonged to the reformist landscapists of the 1620s, but the present was dominated by the high Mannerism of Hendrick Goltzius and his school in Haarlem. Their starting point was the work of the Antwerp-born Bartholomeus Spranger, and Spranger and his pupils became some of the first international superstars, travelling around Europe, working for such courts as those of Albrecht of Bavaria in Munich and the Emperor Rudolf II in Prague. When Goltzius went to Italy for the first time in 1590–91 he was such a famous figure that he chose to travel incognito in order to be left in peace.

The internationalism and stylistic pluralism of the period are difficult to grasp when we look back three and a half centuries later. History is always written by the winners, and Mannerism was the loser against the varieties of classicising Baroque and Dutch naturalism that came to dominate by the middle of the century. By the following century even the greatest connoisseurs, such as Mariette, found it well-nigh impossible to understand why Mannerism had ever been practised, much less why it had been popular. Hence the splendidly dismissive judgement on Bellange (see p. 9) that serves as a motto for this catalogue.

The re-evaluation of Mannerism in general and Bellange in particular has been left to the twentieth century. The pioneering work was done in Austria and Germany after the First World War, but it is only in the past thirty years that it has been possible to admire Bellange's work unreservedly, without the need to make any prefatory apology. The historical record preserves dim echoes of the sensation that he made in the 1610s; he can still cause as great a sensation in the 1990s.

The superb collection of Bellange's etchings shown in this exhibition has been put together over the past twenty-five years. When the collector mentioned that the Carnegie Museum of Art was thinking of arranging a tour in the United States, I was very anxious that it should be shown in the British Museum. The British Museum's own collection dates from the nineteenth century, precisely when Bellange's art was most neglected, and so is weak, as are all other British collections. As a result Bellange's art has never yet been shown to a British public. After London the exhibition will be shown in the United States, then the Rijksmuseum in Amsterdam, and end in the Statens Museum, Copenhagen. The Print Room there is fortunate enough to possess one of the three known complete uniform sets of the series of Apostles, which, through the generosity of its Keeper, Chris Fischer, has been added to the tour to form an almost complete display of Bellange's *oeuvre*. Of the forty-eight prints he made, all but five (known only in one or two impressions) are to be seen here in excellent impressions; all the missing prints are reproduced in this catalogue. Moreover, thanks to the kindness of the Courtauld Institute of Art and the Curator of its Print Room, Sarah Hyde, we can exhibit for the first time the unique working proof of *The Virgin and Child With Cradle* (no. 6).

Even if Bellange's art speaks directly to the modern age, the historical context in which he worked is now long forgotten and known only to specialists. So it was essential to write a catalogue. Bellange was a genius, and no genius can be explained. But he was a real person who lived among others in a certain place and time, and any information about this helps our understanding and hence our appreciation of his art. Neither I nor my collaborator Craig Hartley are specialists in seventeenth-century art; we come to the subject from the background of the study of prints. But fortunately this period and subject have been greatly illuminated by scholars working over the past century. We have tried to digest what has been discovered, define what is not yet known, and offer some suggestions that might fill in the gaps. We have made a particular effort to explain the subject matter of the prints, as it is essential to understand the stories and personalities that Bellange so dramatically recreates.

We are immensely indebted to the scholars whose researches into the amazingly rich archives in Nancy have laid the foundations for all later writers. Chief among them are Henri Lepage, François-Georges Pariset, Pierre Marot and, most recently, Paulette Choné. Our debt to Paulette Choné is even greater, because she undertook with exceptional kindness to read the typescript of this catalogue. Her numerous observations have saved us from many errors, and we are only sorry that lack of space and time has prevented us from following the many leads she has suggested to us. Needless to say the mistakes that remain are entirely our responsibility.

Bellange's etchings have been studied several times. The standard catalogue, which we have used with much profit, is by Nicole Walch. The best study in English was written by Amy Worthen and Sue Welsh Reed for an exhibition in America in 1974–5. It remains an excellent introduction which we have tried to emulate. In 1994 Sue Reed wrote the Bellange entries for the catalogue of the exhibition *The French Renaissance in Prints*, and we only undertook the present catalogue after she had made it clear that she was unable to do so. We are grateful to her for her advice and much help in our work. A further scholar whose writings have greatly stimulated our thinking is Jacques Thuillier, who contributed the sections on Bellange to the 1992 Nancy exhibition on *L'Art en Lorraine au temps de Jacques Callot*.

One area in which we have been able to advance on our predecessors is in the study of the watermarks of the papers used for Bellange's etchings. This section (pp. 125–40) contains the first set of photographs of Bellange's watermarks that has yet been published. That it has been possible is thanks to the development in very recent years of a new method of 'soft' X-radiography that makes such photography much faster and more practicable. There are certainly many more watermarks to be recorded; when more museums have this equipment it will be possible to come to much more definite conclusions. At present it is only in the Rijksmuseum (where the method was developed) and in the British Museum that the equipment is installed and most of the photographs used have been made in these two institutions. The British Museum owes its equipment to the generosity of the Josefowitz family and to the advice and help of our colleagues in Amsterdam.

On behalf of all the institutions showing this exhibition I would like to express our thanks to the Josefowitz family for so generously making their Bellange collection available for the enjoyment of a wide public. Both I and Craig Hartley wish to add our personal thanks for their many kindnesses during the writing of this catalogue. We have many other debts to colleagues and friends. In the first place we thank the curators of the institutions in which we have studied; many are individually acknowledged in the section on watermarks but we are grateful to all. We also thank the Philadelphia Museum of Art, the Museum of Fine Arts in Boston and the Kupferstichkabinett in Berlin for permission to reproduce their photographs of unique impressions in their collections; the photographs of prints in the British Museum and the Josefowitz collection were taken by Graham Javes and James Rossiter. We thank our collaborators, Linda Batis, Chris Fischer and Ger Luijten, for their help in arranging the tour. Lastly, but not least, we thank all the other scholars who helped us in writing the catalogue: Peter Barber, John Gash, Robert Gerard, Richard Godfrey, Jean-Michel Massing and Nicholas Penny.

ANTONY GRIFFITHS

Introduction

'Bellange is one of those painters whose licentious manner, completely removed from a proper style, deserves great distrust. It nevertheless had its admirers, and Bellange had a great vogue … Several pieces by him are known, which one cannot bear to look at, so bad is their taste.'

Pierre-Jean Mariette (1694–1774)

The essential facts that are known about Jacques Bellange (c.1575–1616) can be quickly laid out. He first turns up in the archives of the ducal court in Nancy in 1602, when he was engaged as one of the court painters of Duke Charles III. From then onwards his name regularly appears in the court accounts, either when he received his salary (usually years in arrears) or when he was paid for some specific commission. There are some 140 references in all to him between 1602 and 1616, many of which are multiple records of the same payment. Late in 1616 he disappears from the accounts, and a marginal note in them states that he died in that year. Before 1602 his career is a complete blank except for a single document which was discovered and published for the first time in 1981. According to this, Bellange 'living at present in La Mothe' (in the south of the duchy) took on an apprentice in Nancy in 1595. Presumably he must have been at least twenty to have been in a position to do this; it is for this reason that he is now usually considered to have been born in about 1575.

So much for the documents. Reconstructing his output presents different problems. The starting point are his etchings, all but a few of which have his name on the plate. It is now generally accepted that he made forty-eight of them; Bellange's style is so idiosyncratic and unusual in the history of etching that there is little room for argument, and only one or two plates have ever been the subject of disagreement. The opposite is true of his drawings. Here confusion reigns. Several hundred drawings have at some time or other been attributed to him, and no one has published an attempt to define the corpus of those he really drew.[1] A few are preparatory studies for his prints and are unquestionably by him. To this group others can be added on stylistic grounds. But beyond this trouble looms. There were other draughtsmen in France at the time whose drawings look very much like his, and

the task of sorting out and identifying their work has as yet barely begun.[2]

If the drawings present a big problem, Bellange's paintings create an even greater one. His documented works made for the ducal palace in Nancy all disappeared centuries ago, so nothing can be proven to be by him. Into the resulting void has been poured a mass of paintings that have been optimistically attributed to him. The most obvious feature they share is that they are not by the same hand, are not very good and no two scholars can agree on the correctness of their attribution. There is one pair of panels with the head and shoulders of the Virgin and Angel of the Annunciation now in Karlsruhe, which actually bear an old inscription that they are by Bellange, but they are so unattractive that little attention has been paid to them in recent literature. The painting that has been most discussed since it was first published in 1973 is a *Lamentation over the Dead Christ*, now in the Hermitage. The attribution is supported by the existence of a drawing of the same composition that has a good claim to be by Bellange. But the Hermitage painting is rather a nasty object, with lurid flesh tones, and many have refused to believe that it could be from Bellange's hand. The next most plausible candidate is an altarpiece of *Saint Francis in Ecstasy Supported by Two Angels*, now in the Musée Historique Lorrain in Nancy. Its provenance is however unknown. This is a much better painting, but if it is by Bellange it is still a great disappointment to those who love his etchings and expect something equally wonderful from his paintings.[3] Of his abundantly documented activity as a portraitist, nothing survives or at least has yet been attributed to him.

Otherwise we have only a few engravings made after his designs by Crispin de Passe in Cologne in 1600 or 1601. These, as will be seen, are of considerable importance, although perhaps insufficient attention has yet been paid to them.

Modern art historians, nurtured on the wealth of surviving works and of information in Italian and Netherlandish archives in the early seventeenth century, have regarded this poverty of material as something of a mystery. Those who have tried to find out something about British art of these years will, in turn, regard the amount of information surviving as a positive *embarras de richesses*. Some, particularly French historians living in Paris, have regarded Bellange's location in Nancy as particularly problematic: how could one of the finest artists of the day come out of a provincial backwater such as Lorraine? This might seem to be easily answered by stating that no region could be a backwater that gave birth to four such artists as Bellange, the etcher Jacques Callot, and the painters Claude Lorrain and Georges de la Tour. But then when these four are placed next to each other, and the utter dissimilarity of their art becomes manifest, one wonders what sort of school of art it was that Lorraine produced. So the starting point of this essay has to be Lorraine and its capital, the city of Nancy.

The Duchy of Lorraine

Modern Lorraine is a region in the north-east of France, comprising all or parts of the four *départements* of Meuse, Meurthe-et-Moselle, Moselle and, to the south, Vosges. To the north the limit is the German frontier and the Mosel valley with Trier standing at its head. To the south and south-east are the Vosges mountains. To the east is Alsace and its capital Strasbourg, now a French *département*, but once mainly German-speaking and between 1871 and 1919 part of Germany. To the west the road lies open to the heart of France. Nancy itself lies about 150 miles (240 km) to the east of Paris.

In the early seventeenth century the status of Lorraine was utterly different. Although French-speaking, it was not part of France at all. It was an autonomous duchy, whose dukes for many centuries had been subject to the Holy Roman Emperor to whom they owed fealty. But in practice most dukes played little heed to the Emperor, and often performed a precarious balancing act between the Kingdom of France to the west and the disparate mass of German lands of the Empire to the east. It had its own laws, its own lower courts, its own local administration and its own currency.

The explanation of this situation, as of most of the political geography of Europe over the past millennium, goes back to the division of Charlemagne's Empire after his death in 814. Between France and Germany lay a block of land that ran from north to south along the left bank of the Rhine. This was the old Kingdom of Lothair, or Lotharingia in Latin, whence the name Lorraine is derived. This area later broke up into many smaller principalities, which were gradually whittled away by pressure from both sides. Each of these small areas was a patchwork of sub-terrains each with its own jurisdiction and feudal rights. It was a world that defeats cartography and that was swept away by the military victories and legal revolution of Napoleon in the early nineteenth century. Today the only traces of the old European patchwork lie in such tiny principalities as Liechtenstein, Andorra, Monaco and San Marino, and in the much larger Grand Duchy of Luxembourg.

The Duchy of Lorraine that Bellange knew was itself a composite of parts. To the east was Lorraine proper, with Nancy as its capital. To the west was the Duchy of Bar, also held by the Duke of Lorraine. This in turn was divided into two areas with different legal status: the *Barrois mouvant* and the *Barrois non mouvant*. Within the overall area there were three independent bishoprics, those of Metz, Verdun and Toul, which were notionally part of the German Empire but were in fact firmly under the control of the King of France, who occupied them with military garrisons from 1552. From this date their inhabitants were considered, by

Fig. 1 Crispin de Passe (*c.*1565–1637), *Charles III of Lorraine*, engraving 1594. 148 × 113 mm (oval). British Museum

the French at least, as citizens of France. The three bishoprics owned patches of land scattered throughout the region.

For well over a century the political history of Lorraine was determined by three dukes: Charles III (1543–1608), his son Henri II (1563–1624) and Henri's nephew Charles IV (1604–75). They fall into the classic pattern of the wise, creative first generation, the weak and indolent second, and the rash and extravagant third. Charles III (fig. 1) built up Lorraine, Henri II (fig. 2) maintained it, and Charles IV (fig. 19) destroyed it. Travellers in the early seventeenth century were amazed by the wealth and prosperity of the country. Ten years into the Thirty Years' War Lorraine was a disaster area: a third of the population had died, plague was endemic and the survivors were reduced to penury. These were the years of Callot's *Miseries of War*, published in 1636, the year after Callot's sudden death at the age of forty-two from causes that are now unknown but that were presumably connected with the troubles of those years. It was not until the end of the century that Lorraine recovered its former prosperity with the restoration of the royal house. In 1736 Lorraine finally became part of France, after Duke Francis III swapped it for the Grand Duchy of Tuscany; in 1745 he was elected Holy Roman Emperor as Francis I.

During and after the sixteenth century the German Empire was in the hands of the Habsburgs and, although the imperial branch based in Prague (or after 1612 Vienna) was no threat, the Spanish branch was of great importance. Lorraine lay between two Spanish possessions, the Netherlands and the Franche-Comté. A war had been going on in the Netherlands since the revolt against the Spanish in the 1560s, and Lorraine was near the chief supply route for the Spanish. The French naturally regarded the surrounding Spanish presence with great foreboding, and this hostility determined much of French foreign policy. It was perhaps inevitable that Lorraine should get caught up in this and that the establishment of French supremacy over Spain should lead first to the occupation of Lorraine and eventually to its absorption into France.

The links between the courts of Lorraine and France were always close. Charles III inherited the duchy as a two-year-old in 1545, and was himself brought up at the French court from 1552 onwards. He was lucky as well as able. When he returned to take up his dukedom in Nancy in 1559, France was about to slide into the anarchy of the civil wars that pitted Catholics against Huguenot Protestants. In 1559 Charles married Claude,

Fig. 2 Thomas de Leu (*c.*1555–1611/12), *Henri II of Lorraine*, engraving *c.*1599. 208 × 143 mm. British Museum

the daughter of the French King Henri II and his Italian wife Catherine de' Medici. His second cousins were the Guise family, the most powerful family in France at the time and the leaders of the Catholic League (and much disliked by the French for being 'foreigners'). So for a few decades the Kings of France were no threat to Lorraine. It was Charles himself who in the 1580s revived an old claim of the Dukes of Lorraine to the French throne, perhaps the only major mistake of his career as it led to an invasion of Lorraine in 1587 by an army of Lutheran soldiers. The undisputed grasp of Henri IV on the French throne after his conversion to Catholicism led to a treaty with Lorraine in 1593, which was followed in 1599 by the marriage of Henri, Charles's heir, to Catherine, the Protestant sister of Henri IV. It was for her that Bellange is first recorded as working in 1602.

Lorraine was a stronghold of Catholic orthodoxy, and Protestants were never allowed to live in Nancy, or

Fig. 3 Anonymous (Matthaeus Merian?), *Henri II and Marguerite of Gonzaga*, etching *c*.1612. 130 × 103 mm. British Museum

preach or practise their religion. This meant that Lorraine was spared any internal replay of the struggles that had torn France apart, although it made the position of the hapless Catherine virtually impossible, disliked both by her husband and by the populace. After she died childless in 1604, Henri remarried in 1606 Margarita (Marguerite) of Gonzaga from Mantua (fig. 3). This marriage was part of a pattern of Italian alliances that Lorraine shared with France. As Henri II had married Catherine de' Medici and Henri IV married Marie de' Medici, so Charles III's daughter Christine married the Grand Duke of Tuscany, Ferdinando de' Medici. Of his other two daughters, one, Antoinette, married the Duke of Cleves, while the other, Elisabeth, married Maximilian I of Bavaria. Members of the ducal family often travelled around Europe. Between September and December 1603 Charles visited his son-in-law Maximilian of Bavaria in Munich; there is evidence that a painter, probably Danglus, was among his retinue.[4] For several months in late 1620 and early 1621 the future Charles IV of Lorraine visited his aunt Christine in Florence, an event that modern historians have sometimes linked

to Callot's return to Nancy later in 1621. All these connections, to which must be added the strong Spanish presence to the north and south, helped create a cosmopolitan court culture in Nancy.

This is a fact of fundamental importance for understanding Bellange. Lorraine was not part of France, and its artists were not French. When one of them, Georges Lallemand, settled in Paris, he only became a naturalised French citizen at the very end of his life, because, as a foreigner, his entire estate would have become the property of the French crown on his death. When French armies occupied Nancy, Callot held out to the last possible moment before swearing a compulsory oath of fealty to the French king, and refused to make a print commemorating the siege and capture of Nancy itself. Artists in Lorraine knew what was happening in France; Bellange himself was given a travel grant by Charles III in 1608 to see what was being done in Paris. But they equally looked in other directions. Callot was trained in Rome and made his early career in Florence. Claude stayed in Rome all his life. Many others went to Italy, and all knew well the abundant production of prints that was pouring from the presses across Europe. Lorraine was not a province, and its artists were not provincial. Even three centuries later, after the absorption of Lorraine into France, Nancy retained its artistic independence. It was the home of French *art nouveau*, the town where the glassmaker Emile Gallé and the furniture-maker Louis Majorelle made their careers.

Nancy

It is fortunate for us that the Nancy of Bellange's day is preserved in one of the most beautiful town views of the early seventeenth century. This is the two-plate etching (fig. 4) by Friedrich Brentel that was made for Claude de la Ruelle in 1611, and published as part of a famous series on the funeral of Charles III and the accession of Henri II – a series to which we shall return (p. 26).

On the left is the old town, with its medieval street pattern, dominated by the mass of the ducal palace. On the right is the Ville-Neuve, the new town laid out according to the most up-to-date Italian ideas by the Neapolitan Giambattista Stabili. Whereas the old town was centuries old, the new town was founded by Charles III in 1588. The brief incursion of German soldiers in 1587 had done a great deal of damage, and revealed the insecurity of Nancy itself. So the first priority was to strengthen the walls and rebuild the fortifications of the old town. This work had already begun in 1553 and was carried out by a series of Italian engineers; it was pursued with great urgency after 1587 and was complete by about 1600. The cost was enormous, but Charles succeeded in making Nancy one of the best protected cities in Europe. As can be seen in the view by Brentel, the old town was completely fortified in itself, with only a narrow passage allowing access to and from the new town. The new town was also given its own ring of walls, which were built by Stabili between 1603 and 1610, and which were regarded at the time as the finest in the world. The streets were laid out according to the plans of Charles and Stabili, and plots in it were sold to individuals and religious foundations on condition that they build on them. This income helped pay for the costs of fortifying the new town itself. The new town was a great success, and by 1628 had 16,000 inhabitants.[5]

Nancy was not a large town; it was, for example, smaller and of more recent origin than the neighbouring Metz. It was a political rather than a commercial or intellectual capital, and most of the inhabitants were connected to the court, either directly or as suppliers of goods and services. Its very large numbers and extravagant scale could only be supported because of the prosperity of the dukes themselves, whose wealth was founded on their control of the minerals of the country; the largest income came from the lead and salt mines. Charles III pursued a consciously mercantilist policy of building up local manufactures in the new town. A writer in 1617 recorded: 'In this city are artisans from all countries attracted by the gifts, exemptions and immunities that Charles has given to encourage them to settle there. These trades were previously unknown in Lorraine, such as gold beaters, silk weavers and dyers, manufacturers of cauldrons and other articles of copper, polishers and cutters of marble, soap makers; as well as masters of other arts such as architects, cutters of diamonds, rubies and other stones, painters, sculptors, statuaries, embroiderers and expert tapestry weavers.'[6] Evidence about many of these people survives. For instance in 1604 Charles asked his sister the Duchess of Brunswick to persuade a tapestry-maker to come from Brussels to Nancy to 'demonstrate the art of tapestry'; two such tapestry-makers appear on plate 16 of his funeral procession. He supported an engraver on crystal, Claude Parise, at more or less the same time as Rudolf II in Prague gave a patent for the technique to Caspar Lehmann, who is now remembered while Parise is forgotten.[7]

Parallels with the court culture in Prague can also be found in the reign of Henri II, who shared Rudolf's fascination with alchemy and other semi-scientific pursuits. One of those involved in the experiments was Jean La Hiere, the architect responsible for the perspectives in the funeral of Charles III.[8] Duke Henri was also interested in astronomy. In 1610 he commissioned from Stabili (who was also a gifted mathematician) an extraordinary plan for an astronomical laboratory to be sited outdoors in the upper parterre of the palace garden. It was never completed, although two bronze globes were made. It is no coincidence that he had this idea at exactly the same time as Galileo dedicated his first astronomical observations, the *Siderus Nuncius* (Starry Messenger) of 1610, to Henri's brother-in-law, Cosimo II de' Medici.[9]

Despite the commercial interests in the new town, Nancy must still have been dominated by the court and by the numerous religious establishments in the city. The numbers of the latter were startling. Besides the churches, there were thirty-two convents, abbeys and priories; not surprisingly the town was referred to as a *ville couvent*. From these emerged some leading figures of the Catholic Counter-Reformation. Charles campaigned to establish Nancy as an episcopal see, and although Pope Clement VII did not grant this, a primatial chapter was established in Nancy by papal Bull on 15 March 1602. The Ville-Neuve was extended in order to accommodate the building of a new primatial church, and the title was given to Charles's son, Cardinal Charles de Lorraine (1567–1607), who was already Bishop of Metz and Prince-Bishop of Strasbourg.[10] There were many schools in Nancy but no establishment of higher education. The closest university was to be found at Pont-à-Mousson, 20 miles (32 km) further north, where it had been founded by Charles III in 1572. This was another Catholic stronghold and was run by the Jesuit Order.

In the early seventeenth century the court consisted of over 350 persons as well as forty-two Swiss soldiers in the royal guard. It was housed in a complex of buildings that can be seen both in the Brentel view and, in more detail, in a large etching by Claude Deruet made in 1641. The chief buildings can easily be distinguished. The oldest part is the long gallery, the Galerie des Cerfs, which stretches along the main street and was decorated with a celebrated cycle of paintings by the court painter Hughes de la Faye between 1524 and 1529. These juxtaposed large scenes of the life of deer with small roundels containing scenes from the life of Christ; the parallels between the life of the deer and of Christ (for example, the Nativity with the birth of the

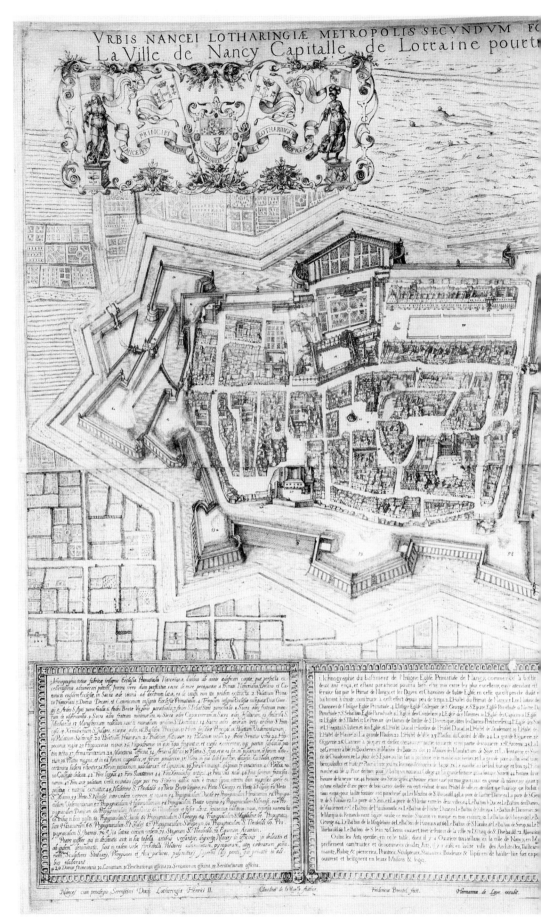

Fig. 4 Friedrich Brentel (1580–1651), *Plan of Nancy*, etching 1611. 696 × 927 mm. British Museum

Fig. 5 Jacques Callot (1592–1635), *The Parterre of the Palace of Nancy*, etching 1625. 248 × 392 mm. British Museum

fawn) were explained by French texts.[11] Documents show that Bellange was commissioned to repaint these in 1606, but the gallery, after much neglect, was burnt in 1871 and whatever was left on the walls was destroyed. This is the single wing that survives of the entire palace, and today houses the Musée Historique Lorrain.

To the left of fig. 4 is the Franciscan Church of the Cordeliers, founded by René II in 1477. Between 1609 and 1615, following the death of Charles III in 1608, a royal sepulchre, designed by Stabili and Jean Richier, was built on to the north side of the apse. It was circular in ground-plan and was inspired by the Cappella dei Principi, the funerary chapel of the Medici family added on to San Lorenzo in Florence, which had been planned from the 1560s but only actually begun in 1605.

Other parts of the ducal palace are today familiar from the etchings of Jacques Callot. The garden behind, the famous Parterre (fig. 5), was built as part of the construction of the new fortifications. It fell into an upper and lower part, and the 1611 view of Nancy (fig. 4) shows that it was essentially complete by then. Later in 1616 fourteen stone statues in niches in the wall between the lower and upper halves were carved by the court sculptor Simon Drouin. To the north-east, the long street leading towards the new town is the Carrière of Nancy. This still survives, although all the façades of the houses were refaced in the eighteenth century when King Stanislas Leszczynski of Poland gave the city the Rococo finish and the spectacular decorative ironwork gates and screens by Jean Lamour that are responsible for so much of its beauty today.

Art in Lorraine

To discuss painting in Lorraine in the years before and during the life of Bellange is a peculiar business. The losses have been catastrophic, and no wall paintings and very few canvases have survived. What is more, those that have survived are usually undocumented, and their attribution is disputed. So we have very little idea what the paintings of any particular artist looked like; it is only after Bellange's death that things begin to be clarified. On the other hand the documentation about the artists who worked there is exceptionally good by French standards. The main royal archives in Paris were destroyed by a fire in 1737, and so little is known of what was going on there. The court archives of Lorraine survive more or less complete from 1476 to 1737, with interruptions in 1635–61 and 1670–98 caused by French occupations. They include all the accounts of the income and expenditure of the dukes, often including original invoices from the suppliers. The total number of registers is about 9,200.[12]

As a result we know a great deal about what the court painters were commissioned to do for the dukes. There are no equivalent archives for the various religious foundations, and so the information about non-ducal commissions that were given to painters is far less complete. This probably distorts our understanding of their work. In the case of Bellange we know a great deal about his ducal commissions and nothing about any others. They may have existed; they may not.

What then is the picture that emerges from the ducal accounts of artistic activity in Nancy? From early in the sixteenth century there is a clear succession of painters in the service of the Dukes of Lorraine; as one died another was appointed to take his place. Often there were two of them, but this number could rise to as many as four at certain times. Each artist was paid an annual retainer of 100 or 200 francs. Fees for specific works were paid on top of this. A strong dynastic element can be traced in the succession of names. This tradition is worth describing because it shows how far Bellange's career stood apart from the normal pattern.[13]

Let us take up the sequence in the middle of the sixteenth century, when the two court painters were Claude Crocq and Médard Chuppin, successors to Hughes de la Faye who had died in 1539. The two men received their appointments around 1540, and in 1545 were sent together to Italy by the duke in order to improve their knowledge and expertise. They were there for no less than five years, and on their return were shown marks of great favour. In 1556 Crocq was raised to the nobility, and Chuppin received the same honour eleven years later. When Chuppin was married in 1559, the duke gave him a present of 500 francs.

Both men had sons who followed them into the profession of artist. Crocq died in 1572, leaving a son Balthasar still a child. The duke adopted him, and in 1581 sent him to Italy for further training. After his return he was raised to the nobility in 1585, and appointed a herald of arms. Something must have gone wrong, for in 1600 he lost his position, and was replaced two years later by Jean Callot, the father of the famous etcher Jacques. Jacques was himself apprenticed in 1607 to Demenge Crocq, a die engraver who made the coinage for the Dukes of Lorraine. It is not known whether or how he was related to the other Crocqs. But the name is an odd one and it seems most unlikely that in a small society such as Nancy there were two unrelated Crocq families.

Chuppin lived eight years longer than Crocq, dying in 1580 leaving two sons. The younger Nicolas, who lived into the 1620s, appears to have been little more than a decorator, but his elder brother Charles held a position as painter to the duke between 1589 and 1625, and often collaborated with Claude Henriet (c.1540–1603), the leading painter of the years immediately before Bellange. He was brought from Paris by Charles III in 1586. It was Henriet's son Israel who was in Italy with Callot and who later settled in Paris, where he acted as Callot's publisher.

Two further names appear in the accounts as ducal painters around the turn of the century. The earlier is Jean de Wayembourg, who worked in Nancy from 1592 until his death in 1603. The next is Jean Danglus, who was Bellange's collaborator in the first contract he received in 1602 after obtaining his position as court artist.

Before examining the documents on Bellange himself, it is worth asking what these artists were actually expected to do. The answer, as it appears from the court accounts, is rather surprising to modern expectations. They made few freestanding paintings of the sort that we would find in a modern art gallery. Those that were painted were the portraits of members of the court that were either hung in official buildings or were sent around the world as presents to further some diplomatic goal. The main task of the ducal painters was to undertake what would now be described as decorative schemes. They painted the woodwork and the walls of rooms with friezes and grotesques. One of the more ambitious projects was to paint a map of the duke's territories; one of the least was to paint the balusters of the bed of the queen dowager and the street signs for the Ville-Neuve.[14] They had to supply innumerable coats of arms for display in the palace and paint flags for military companies and for the court tournaments. The court frequently staged masques and carnivals. For these the artists had not only to paint all the apparatus but also to provide designs for the costumes; the court tailors turned these into actual clothes. The only documented surviving works by any sixteenth-century Lorrainese artist are five drawings by Médard Chuppin for costumes for a festival held in 1580.[15] Finally artists were called upon for entries of state, funerals and other occasions of political import.

Charles III had a reputation as a cultivated man. But there is no sign anywhere that he tried to rival any of his contemporaries as a collector or patron. His cousins, the Guise family, were outstanding patrons and the main employers of Primaticcio after the King of France.[16] Charles is not known to have collected paintings by artists of either his own or previous generations, although a *galerie des peinctures* in the ducal palace had been created before 1606.[17] Unfortunately we have no idea what was hung in it. Charles does not seem to have been a significant collector, unlike many contemporary princes who created famous cabinets of curiosities of a wide range. He did inherit from Duke Antoine in the early sixteenth century a collection of *singularitez*, and in 1599 paid the extraordinary price of 60,000 florins for a unicorn's horn, an object that was thought to cure illness and neutralise poison.[18] His painters, although well paid and treated, did not rank high in the court hierarchy. In the accounts they are placed among the artisans, and paid the same. In the procession at his funeral the artists were given no special place; the court tailors and mint workers were. The fact that artists were sent to Italy or Paris at ducal expense does not mean that the duke had grand ideas about them. It simply implies that he did not want visiting royalty from abroad to think that the festivals and entertainments that were provided for them lagged behind internationally acceptable standards.

Of course there is no reason to think that the painters saw themselves in these restricted terms. The very fact that they had travelled meant that they had seen the exceptional status that painters could hold. Ever since the achievements of Raphael, Michelangelo and Titian it had been clear that a great painter could be recognised as a genius and be regarded with awe by princes and fellow-artists alike. The currency of such ideas is found in a sonnet by Jean de Rosière, which contains the only literary reference to Bellange dating from his lifetime.[19] In it Bellange is credited with wishing to make a masterpiece in order to make his name immortal, like Apelles, Zeuxis and Parrhasius. The impossibility of playing such an exalted role in Nancy must have been the driving force behind Bellange's ambitious programme of making himself known to the entire world through printmaking.

The occasion of the writing of de Rosière's flattering sonnet was the painting of a portrait of Marguerite of Gonzaga, shortly after her arrival in Lorraine in 1606, by Bellange himself. The experience of this sitting may lie behind a remark she made in a letter she sent back to her relations in Mantua in about 1608; here in Nancy, she said, there are no good painters.[20] Humiliations such as these can only have strengthened Bellange's determination to escape from his surrounds.

Documents on Bellange's Life

A complete listing of all the documents in the Nancy court archives that refer to Bellange is of interest only to specialists. Here will be singled out only those that throw light on the work he did officially for the court. This is now completely lost but is the background for his etchings, none of which had anything to do with his official functions and none of which is mentioned in the court accounts.

The first contract that Bellange was given on 15 October 1602 was to paint with Jacques Danglus a room in the ducal palace for Catherine of Bourbon (fig. 6), who had married Henri, the heir to the dukedom three years earlier. This was for a cycle of twelve paintings, six from Roman history and six of devices 'at the pleasure of Madame'. In addition they were to decorate the rest of the woodwork in the room. For this work, which was finished in April 1603, Bellange was paid 1080 francs. His engagement as a court painter followed a week after this contract. His annual retainer was 400 francs – a surprisingly high figure and twice what any court painter before him had been paid. In the court hierarchy he ranked below Wayembourg, but above Charles Chuppin, Claude Henriet and one Julien Le Maire. The following year Wayembourg and Henriet both died, Le Maire disappeared by 1607, Danglus (chiefly a portraitist) is last mentioned in 1610, and only Charles Chuppin was left. Chuppin's ability seems to have been small, and in the accounts he usually appears as a heraldic painter.[21] As a result Bellange's position as the premier artist of the court was secure within a few years of his joining it.

In the following years he was given some commissions for rather unusual kinds of painting. Besides the predictable court portraits, he was paid for a Mary Magdalene and a Saint Francis; this may not seem very revealing, but it is one of the very few cases when the subject of any painting by any artist is specified in the court accounts. In 1604 the sixteen-year-old Claude

Deruet, the son of a Nancy clockmaker, was apprenticed to him for a term of four years for a fee of 200 francs. This was the man who was to succeed to Bellange's place as the leading Nancy painter in the 1620s. He was a friend of Callot, who made a well-known portrait etching of him, and he dominated art in the city until his death in 1660.[22] Georges de La Tour (1593–1652), his contemporary, had nothing like the same success, and worked most of his life in Vic and Lunéville, having very little connection with Nancy.

In 1606 Bellange was given two big contracts. The first was to repaint the Galerie des Cerfs, the principal public space in the ducal palace which stretched along the main street. It had first been painted by Hugues de La Faye and others in the 1520s, but suffered badly from damp.[23] In 1598–1600 Claude Henriet, Remond Constant and a certain Moyse Bougault were paid for 'repairing the effaced paintings' in the gallery. But this had not solved the problem, which was of real importance as the gallery was the largest in the palace and

Fig. 6 Jan Wierix (1549–after 1615), *Catherine of Bourbon*, engraving 1600. 358 × 262 mm. British Museum

much used; it had for many years served as a law court. The contract was for the very large sum of 1200 francs, which implies that Bellange must more or less have repainted the gallery over again; and indeed a document of 1626 refers to the 'Galerie des Cerfs de Bellange'. The payment document states that he had painted twenty scenes of a deer hunt along the two sides of the gallery, a large one on the wall opposite the entrance, a half-size one over the two entrance doors, and three figures of people on the fourth wall, on either side of the fireplace. This description implies that he stuck to the old iconography (see p. 13), even though the small roundels with the life of Christ are not mentioned. Hunting trophies were hung along the walls, and an enormous table with a *pietra dura* top was in the centre.[24]

The second contract was for 1700 francs, and was shared with three other painters, among them Danglus. This was for painting the triumphal arch built for the entry into Nancy of Marguerite of Gonzaga, Henri's new wife whom he had married in 1606 after Catherine's death in 1604. The text of the contract survives and shows that the arch itself, surmounted by a figure of Virgil in homage to Marguerite's Mantuan origins, was designed by the sculptor Florent Drouin. The team was given just over a month to get the thing ready, and Jean Callot provided the painted coats of arms. This was the first time that any such arch had been constructed in Nancy, and shows the ambition to match what was being done elsewhere in Europe. For the ballet that followed this entry Bellange decorated the triumphal chariot, modelling twelve cupids in papier-mâché and painting and gilding the carriage.[25]

Two years later on 5 March 1608, two months before Charles III's death, Bellange was given 135 francs 'to travel into France and study the paintings and other works relevant to his art in the houses, the royal palaces and elsewhere, in order that on his return he may render us even better service in his art, given that our intention is to make particular use of him in this place.' The sum was not large enough for Bellange to spend very long in France, but this is the only document we have that records any travel outside Lorraine. His absence explains why, according to the ducal accounts, he played no part in the designs for the various structures erected for the funeral after the death of Charles III on 14 May 1608. In France he must have seen the recent paintings made for Henri IV by the artists of the so-called Second School of Fontainebleau: Ambroise Dubois, Toussaint Dubreuil and Martin Fréminet. But no one has yet managed to argue convincingly that the work that Bellange saw in France influenced his art in any significant way. The following year the English architect Inigo Jones was sent to Paris from London, ostensibly to carry letters, but in practice to see the remarkable things that were being done by Henri IV.[26] Bellange's visit must be considered in the same light.

The accession of Henri II did not mark any change in Bellange's position. At the end of 1610 he was working on a series of scenes from Ovid's *Metamorphoses* in the Salle Neuve of the duke; around the scenes he was to paint decorative moresques. This was the biggest contract of his career, for which he was paid the very large sum of 4000 francs. He must have used some assistance; a carpenter was paid for erecting scaffolding for 'Bellange and his assistants'. The last payment recorded to him is in 1616 when he received 150 francs for decorating a machine used in a ballet arranged by Marguerite of Gonzaga.

His own position had changed markedly in 1612 when he married Claude Bergeron, the seventeen-year-old daughter of a wealthy Nancy apothecary Pierre. Her dowry was no less than 6000 francs, as well as a promise that the couple should inherit the parents' country estate when they died. Three sons were born in rapid succession, Henri in 1613, Pierre in 1615 and Louis in 1616. The last was baptised on 10 August; within a few months, and certainly before the end of the year, Jacques himself was dead, from causes that are now completely unknown.

The family of Bellange's wife was very well established in Nancy, and much has been learnt about them from surviving documents. Even more has been discovered about his wife Claude. Left widowed at the age of twenty-one, she died over half a century later in 1671 or 1672. She was evidently a bitter and disappointed woman, whose ambitions had been defeated by her husband's death, which had left her with three very young children. Her father had died the year before in 1615, and she was dependent on her mother for maintenance. Eventually she remarried in 1625, when already three months pregnant to the second *valet de chambre* of Duke Charles IV, and had five further children. The children of the first marriage were neglected. Two seem to have died young, but Henri, the eldest, survived and in 1626 at the age of thirteen was apprenticed to Claude Deruet, his father's former apprentice. After living in Rome between 1633 and 1643, he settled in Paris, where he made an undistinguished career for himself as a painter.[27] His mother tried to cut him out of her will, and by an extraordinary chance two letters survive from him addressed to his step-sister in 1672.[28] The cool tone with which he speaks of his late mother shows that their dislike had been mutual.

The central position that Jacques Bellange held in Nancy society is revealed by other documents. He acted as witness at weddings, stood as godparent to the children of friends and took on apprentices. Other relationships are shown by those who acted as witnesses in legal documents concerning Bellange himself. Thus his marriage contract was witnessed by four of the senior officials at the ducal court. When his first son was born in 1613, he was named Henri after Duke Henri II, who stood as godfather at the baptism; Christine de Salm, Countess of Vaudémont, wife of the duke's brother François, acted as godmother. He was evidently a man held in very high regard and with a brilliant future when he suddenly died, at an age that cannot have been much greater than forty. Of the character of the man himself we know nothing. An apothecary's prescription book that happens to survive lists his name frequently as a client between 1607 and 1612. Paulette Choné informs us that the main item was *bolus de casse*, that is, laxative pills. He was also buying turpentine, which might have been used for printmaking as much as medicaments.

One odd phenomenon of the many documents that were produced after Bellange's death is that no relative on his side of the family is ever mentioned, and not a single family connection appears in any document concerning his life. The name Bellange is not otherwise known in Nancy at the time, although there was a small village of this name in Lorraine, near Vic. This is very unusual in a society as close and small as that of Nancy and leads us to the problem of his origins.

His full name, Jacques-Charles de Bellange, is only found on a few documents at the end of his life. More usually (and on all the etchings) he signs himself simply Jacques Bellange. On eight of his prints he adds *Eques* (knight). All modern authorities agree that this title could not have been given him in Lorraine, in which case it must come from another court. This would imply some stage in his career of which we know nothing.[29] At the Nancy court his position was as *gentilhomme suivant son altesse*. This term has a specific meaning. There were two groups of courtiers, those of *l'hôtel* and those of *la chambre: la chambre* meant the duke's personal retainers, while *l'hôtel* was the general court establishment. Painters belonged to the latter group, and in 1603 Bellange was listed as a *valet de garderobe* among them. The fact that he is first recorded in 1602 as a painter working for Catherine of Bourbon has led some scholars to suggest that he came with her from Paris and that he was not therefore a native of Lorraine at all. But this has been shown to be wrong. She had arrived in Nancy in 1599, and it was not until 1602 that Bellange started to work for her. In any event he was actually working for the duke, and his appointment was to the duke's court.[30]

Some light is shed on his origins by a document first published in 1981.[31] According to this, Bellange, a painter 'presently residing at La Mothe' took on an apprentice in Nancy in 1595. One of the witnesses was Jean Blayer de Bariscort the Younger (active 1572–1615), a well-documented Nancy painter, whose name often appears in the ducal accounts for minor works, but who held no court position.[32] La Mothe was a walled village in the south of the Duchy of Bar; it held an important strategic position and was systematically demolished by the French after a siege in 1645. For this reason it will not be found on any modern map. The fact that Bellange went to Nancy to collect an apprentice and the fact that he was recorded as living 'at present' at La Mothe combine to show that he was not a native of that town; in which case he is most likely to have come from Nancy. But in this case who were his parents and why is there no trace of any relations in the records?

This is very odd and demands some explanation. The most reasonable suggestion that has yet been made is that he was illegitimate.[33] If his father was a man of some importance and influence, some of his later career may become more comprehensible. It might help explain how he managed to secure a court position so easily, leaping over long-established dynastic interests.

Documents on Bellange's Etchings

Only one of the many seventeenth-century documents relating to Bellange's career and family makes any mention of his prints. This is a legal document dated 29 July 1619, three years after his death, and was drawn up on behalf of his widow.[34] It lists some of the assets of the estate. Among them were a total of 14,000 francs said to have been owed to Bellange at his death by the duke for various unspecified works done for him. What these might have been is quite unclear, as the very complete court records exclude the possibility that Bellange had been commissioned to do anything like as much work as would produce this enormous figure. Perhaps the art of improving the truth was practised as skilfully in the seventeenth century as it is today, and with the help of her lawyers Bellange's widow had introduced

some significant inflation into the figure between 1616 and 1619 to her own benefit. It did not do her any good, for the so-called debt was never paid.[35]

Other assets were twenty-two copper plates *figurées en plusieurs sortes d'histoires* (with figures from various stories), which were evidently regarded as being valuable. But, the document explains, they could not be valued by painters, as they were not within their field of expertise, nor by expert printers either.[36] There is no reason to think that Bellange owned plates made by anyone else, and the obvious conclusion is that these were the copper plates of Bellange's own etchings. This reveals a fact that is of great importance: Bellange still owned at least some of his copper plates at his death. In 1619 twenty-two of them remained; there may have been more in 1616. Modern cataloguers have reached the conclusion – one that seems entirely correct – that Bellange made a total of forty-eight etched plates. So twenty-six were not there. Some of Bellange's prints are very rare indeed, and only a handful of impressions survive, and these must be from among the twenty-six missing plates. Other prints are relatively common, and these must conversely be among the survivors.

But before developing this argument further, some explanation must be given of the art and technique of etching, and of how prints were marketed in the early seventeenth century. The art of etching has remained unchanged to the present day, so the first part of the following account is true in its broad outlines for all etchings. But the way in which they are sold has changed out of all recognition, and all presumptions based on twentieth-century methods of marketing must be discarded.

The Art of Etching

The materials needed for etching are a polished copper plate, a needle, wax and acid. The plate is covered with the wax, and lines are drawn through it with the needle so as to expose the underlying copper. The plate is then immersed in a bath of acid long enough for the acid to eat into the exposed lines to the desired depth; this operation can be repeated several times. The plate is then taken out of the acid and the wax cleaned off the surface. It is now ready for printing.

A copper-plate printing press looked rather like an old-fashioned clothes mangle (see fig. 7). There were two wooden rollers turned by a manually operated wheel; between them pass a board on which the plate is placed face upwards, covered by a sheet of paper and

21

some soft blankets. The plate has to be inked first: this is done by warming it and dabbing a thick printing ink onto the surface and working it into all the lines etched into the plate so that they are completely full of ink. The surplus ink has to be cleaned off the surface of the plate by rubbing it with a succession of muslin cloths, taking care not to press too hard so that ink is not dragged out of the lines, yet taking equal care that the surplus ink is taken off the surface. A light film can be left in order to provide a light tone on the paper ('surface tone'), or the surface can be wiped completely clean so that the paper remains white. In this condition the plate is ready for printing. The printing paper needs to be thoroughly dampened so that, when the plate and paper pass together through the rollers of the press, all the ink is pulled out of the lines and transferred onto the surface of the paper. The blankets ensure that the pressure of

Fig. 7 Anonymous, *An Etching Press* (from V. Zonca, *Novo Teatro di Machine*, 1621 edition), etching. 246 × 153 mm. British Library

the rollers is even and that no part of the plate prints darker than another.

We know only a limited amount about the exact materials that Bellange would have used. None of his plates survives to the present day, but from others of the period such as Callot's (many of which survive in the Musée Historique Lorrain) it is clear that fairly thick sheets of copper were used. Making these was a laborious and expensive operation: copper itself is dear, and the processes of repeated hammering and reworking that are necessary to make it flat are time-consuming. But they are essential: any flaw or hole in the plate, however trivial, will hold ink in the wiping, and so will print as a dot or blot and interfere with the artist's composition. Some of the random and unintended spots seen in Bellange's prints are due to this cause. Lorraine was a centre of mining, and the brother of one of Bellange's patrons owned a copper-beating factory in the Ville-Neuve which was awarded a monopoly (see no. 3). In the contract for the *Funeral of Charles III* (see p. 27) it is carefully specified that the printer should supply the plates (to satisfy himself with their quality) but that the bills (obviously large) should be settled by La Ruelle (the court official) himself. Later in the century the best copper plates were said to come from Hungary.[37]

The next most important material was the etching ground. This has been loosely described as 'wax' above but is in fact a more complicated amalgam of various materials. Each etcher seems to have had his own favourite ground, and early etching manuals give various recipes for their composition. The acid used was also important, as it has to work together with the ground. Otherwise the acid will bite indiscriminately (what is known as 'foul-biting') and the plate and all the hours spent drawing on it will be wasted.

No etching press from as early as the seventeenth century survives, but they are illustrated in prints from the 1560s onwards, and these give a good idea how they were built (see fig. 7).[38] They were made entirely of wood, without any metal elements. One might have thought that warping would have been a threat and that keeping an even pressure must have been a constant problem. But the quality and evenness of early prints is such as to show that the printers of the day were fully masters of their trade. No changes made in the three and a half centuries since Bellange's day have improved the quality of prints, although they might have made the life of the printer easier.

One great advantage enjoyed by all printers working before the end of the eighteenth century was the availability of the most excellent paper. Any spectator of this exhibition will see immediately that the paper has survived three and a half centuries in amazingly good condition. Very few sheets show any browning, foxing or any of the other ailments that we have become so accustomed to finding in paper of the past 150 years. This is because of the materials that were used: nothing but linen rags, pure water and size (a glue-like solution used to stiffen paper so that it holds ink).

This art of papermaking was the only one practised in Europe between the fourteenth and eighteenth centuries but is now utterly obsolete and used only for a tiny production for special, usually artistic, purposes. The linen rags came from old clothes (this was before the time of cotton or synthetic fibres), which were beaten into pulp by huge hammers driven by water-wheels. Into this vat of pulp the papermaker scooped his tray; this was made with four slats of wood round the outside, between which was held a grid of crossed wires. These wires give the pattern of crossed lines that can be seen in old 'laid' paper: the vertical 'chainlines' are usually set about an inch apart, and the horizontal 'wiremarks' weave in and out between them. Some further remarks on paper are given in the section on watermarks (pp. 125–6).

The other asset that Bellange could rely on in his printmaking was an excellent ink. Very little study has as yet been given to printing inks of the period, and we only have fragments of information.[39] But one that has been published very recently from mid-sixteenth-century Paris is of great interest, as it is not too remote either in time or place from Bellange. This document proves that some of the main printmakers of the day had their wives make their ink for them and that new batches were supplied every day.[40] It was evidently highly skilled work, and the right sort of lampblack and oil had to be mixed to the right consistency. The results were superb, and even today French printing inks have an unrivalled reputation.

This account of the processes of etching is very summary but should be enough to reveal some of the technical factors that produce problems for the non-professional – and Bellange, a painter by training, was definitely a non-professional as a printmaker. In the first place no one can make an etching without technical instruction. He has to be told how to do it and to have access to the right materials. He may be able to make up his own ground and acid, but he certainly needs to purchase copper plates. He may do the biting of his plates himself, but he may prefer to leave it to an

expert professional. He may find that after he has bitten the plate, cleaned off the ground and printed an impression that he wants to add more lines to it. (This is in fact something that Bellange did the whole time.) In this case he has to lay a second ground on the plate, this time transparent so that he can still see the lines that he originally made. He has to cope with the reversal of his image; the print on paper always comes out in reverse to the drawing on the plate. So a printer probably showed Bellange the trick of taking a counterproof on a clean sheet of paper while the ink of an impression is still wet. (One such counterproof, of Christ in the series of Apostles, survives in the collection in Boston.) After he has finished his design, he may want to add his name to the plate or put some verses underneath. In this case he has to know how to write backwards or else find someone to do it for him.

When the plate is completely finished, his problems are not over. He needs access to a printing press in order to print it, and the printing is a slow and expert business. The plate has to be re-inked and wiped afresh for every impression, and with very large plates, such as *The Adoration of the Magi*, each such inking might well take half an hour. So he has every incentive to leave the printing to a professional printer, of which many existed by the early seventeenth century. He has to acquire the paper, which is expensive. Finally, and not least, he has to sell the impressions in order to recoup his considerable costs.

Print Publishing in the Seventeenth Century

It was the expense of publishing and the difficulty of marketing that provided the dynamics that determined the print world in the Renaissance much as they do today. A very few painters might make prints purely as a hobby and give away the impressions to friends. But most could not afford this luxury. Even if they did not earn their primary income from printmaking, they could not afford to let it become a drag on their finances. The number of etchings that Bellange made and the wide distribution of impressions prove conclusively that he was producing his prints as a business. This means that he had every incentive to print as many impressions as he could sell, and these numbers were potentially large. A well-bitten plate, such as almost all of Bellange's were, would produce many hundreds of impressions before getting badly worn. The only text from the period that offers information on this subject is Zonca's book of 1607, which has already been referred to. He says that an engraved plate will print a thousand impressions before needing retouching; after retouching it will print another thousand. For etchings, however, because the lines are much shallower, Zonca says that the numbers are much lower – perhaps half.[41]

The evidence of many prints of the time proves that, if demand held up, plates were printed until they became so worn as to be ghosts of their former selves. The idea that every impression from a plate should be perfect, and that numbers should be deliberately restricted, is one that never occurs before the nine-teenth century. Its concomitant, the signing and numbering of impressions by the artist in pen or pencil, only starts in the last decades of that century. In the case of Bellange a few plates went on being printed until they were very worn; most, however, are only found in good, unworn, impressions. So the printing runs must have varied considerably, and the evidence of the watermarks shows that some stayed in production much longer than others.

Even five hundred impressions is a large number, and so the primary restriction on the number of impressions that Bellange could have printed was the number that he could sell. Printmakers in his day had two choices. The more commonly chosen option was to sell the plate outright to a professional print publisher. In this way the etcher got an immediate return for his effort. The risk, and the potential profit or loss, rested with some-one else. Alternatively, the artist could retain ownership of his plates and hence possibly derive a much greater profit. But he then had to pay the printer, buy the paper and see to all the details of selling impressions.

The fact that no publishers' names are found on early states of Bellange's prints suggests that he never used a publisher, and the fact that twenty-two plates were still in his estate in 1619 proves that these plates at least had never left his possession. Since there were no print publishers in Nancy he probably had little option. But this makes his decision to turn to printmaking all the more extraordinary.

Printmaking in Lorraine during Bellange's Lifetime

By the second half of the sixteenth century printmaking was a highly developed business, centralised in a few major cities. In Italy they were Rome and Venice; no other towns there played much of a role. In the Netherlands there was Antwerp, which had become the centre of a colossal business that dominated not only the Netherlands but Spain as well. The war and the siege and capture of Antwerp by the Spanish army under Alessandro Farnese in 1585 led most Protestants, over half the population, to leave the city. Among them were many engravers, and this huge diaspora of talented experts directly promoted the spread of print-making in other centres. The growth of the print trade in the northern United Provinces, in cities such as Amsterdam and Haarlem, began in this decade. Other Flemish engravers settled in Germany, especially Cologne and Frankfurt, and in France, primarily in Paris. By the early seventeenth century Parisian printmaking and much of German printmaking was dominated by men of Flemish origin.

In the sixteenth century the two centres of print-making in the French-speaking world were Paris and Lyons. Beyond them there were only a few individuals working in near isolation. Nowhere else does there seem to have been anything that could be called an industry with a base of expertise in engravers and printers, or access to publishers. The situation was particularly bleak in Lorraine. During the sixteenth century there had been two good printmakers who came from Lorraine. The first was Nicolas Beatrizet (b. 1507/15 – d. after 1565), who left for Italy when young and made his entire career in Rome. The other was Pierre Woeiriot (1531/2–99), who was born in Neufchâteau. He made his career initially in Lyons, where he was certainly based in the mid-1550s and again at various times in the 1560s. From about 1557 to 1560 he was in Rome. Otherwise he lived in Damblain, a town very close to La Mothe (see p. 21). In 1557 and between 1561 and 1579 he was paid an annual pension of 100 francs by Charles III as his *imagier* – the term then widely used for printmaker. The duke also gave him particular gifts, the last in 1592. One was in 1561 for a series of thirty-six prints of illustrations to the Old Testament. When it was eventually published in 1580 by Antoine Go, a merchant and French official in Saint-Nicolas-de-Port, the duke gave him another gratuity. In all this the duke was never the starting point; his encouragement seems to have been part of his efforts to promote trade or religion.[42]

In Nancy the situation was very odd. It was only in 1566, more than a century after the invention of letter-press printing, that the first printing press had been installed in the town with the help of a subsidy from the duke,[43] and from then until the end of the century there seems never to have been more than one press in the town, serving local needs. The position with engraving is very confused. After Woeiriot there was indeed some-one who held the position as ducal engraver. This was a certain Alexandre Vallée, born in Bar-le-Duc, who lived between about 1558 and 1626. He received a pension as ducal engraver between 1591 and 1608. What he did in this position for the duke is utterly unclear. Robert-Dumesnil records 142 prints by him, mostly series of prints after Boissard. The range of dates in his signed works goes from 1583 to 1613. Most were made in Metz or Pont-à-Mousson. The only dated ones that state that they were made in Nancy were in 1591–2.[44]

Only slightly less obscure is Jean Appier (about 1565 to before 1620). The first time he is mentioned in the ducal accounts he is called an engineer. Between 1608 and 1610 there are a few engravings bearing his name – a *Virgin and Child* after Parmigianino and a portrait. Five years later is a set of etched plates to illustrate the 1615 and later editions of a book, *Relation journalière du voyage du Levant* of Henri de Beauvau, which had first been published in Toul in 1608; these are far from fine prints. In 1615 he made a contract with a Jewish dealer from Epinal, a town in the Vosges, to sell 500 copies of a work with twelve engravings, the *Seven Penitential Psalms*, presumably engraved by himself. Not a single copy of this survives. The contract describes him as *calcographe entretenu pour le service de son Altesse* (engraver retained in the service of his Grace), but he never held any position at the ducal court. The words in the 1615 contract must be a self-description.[45]

It is his son, Jean Appier the Younger, called Hanzelet (documented between 1612 and 1643), who is the first figure to leave any substantial output. The most recent catalogue of his work lists 165 plates.[46] The earliest surviving print is dated 1617, and thereafter he seems to have maintained a fairly steady production. But Hanzelet never held any position at the Nancy court, and in 1616 left Nancy for Pont-à-Mousson, where he held a new post as the university engraver. His duties in this emanated from the Jesuits, and involved engraving theses, title-pages and illustrations for books, and so on. This was jobbing work of a perfectly respectable but utterly uninteresting kind. He had a side-line as a mathematician and an expert firework pyrotechnist. In 1626 he was described as *maître de feux artificiels en l'artillerie* when he was summoned to Nancy to provide a display on the entry of Charles IV.[47] In 1630 he published a book, *La Pyrotechnie*, in Pont-à-Mousson.

What, it may be asked, about Jacques Callot, who was not only the most famous printmaker that Lorraine

Fig. 8 Jacques Callot (1592–1635), *Charles III of Lorraine*, engraving 1607. 161 × 119 mm. British Museum

ever produced, but one of the greatest printmakers of any age and country? He was born in 1592 in the midst of court circles in Nancy, his father holding the appointment of herald to the dukes. He was apprenticed on 16 January 1607 to a goldsmith, and from this year belongs the single print, a portrait of Charles III, that he made before he left for Rome (fig. 8). Although he must have met Bellange, there is no reason whatever to suggest any professional link between the two men. Callot's training as a printmaker took place in Rome under the engraver and publisher Philippe Thomassin, a Frenchman from Troyes who had long since settled in Italy. Callot lived in Italy for at least a decade, before returning to Nancy at the end of 1620. But it was only three years later, in 1623, that he first appears in the ducal accounts when Henri II began to commission him and also gave him a handsome present on the occasion of his marriage. Only in 1624, after Henri's death, did he begin to describe himself on his plates as *calcographe de son Altesse*.[48]

Surviving letters show that, when Callot did return to

Nancy, his first concern was to get his assistant Antonio Francesco Lucini to follow him from Florence. In Florence Lucini had been described as *factore*, and he was evidently a factotum who helped in preparing plates, printing and selling; a set of copies made by Lucini from Antonio Tempesta is known with his *excudit* ('published') in Nancy.[49] When Lucini returned to Florence,[50] his place was taken by Gatien Aubry, described as *imprimeur et enlumineur en taille-douce* (printer and colourist of engravings), who in 1630 took on an apprentice and witnessed a contract concerning the sale of Callot's plates.[51] Nothing is known about Gatien Aubry's origins, but it may be significant that one of the publishers in Strasbourg for whom Matthaeus Merian worked in 1622 was Peter Aubry.[52] Might Gatien have been a member of the same Aubry family? If so it would support the impression given by the Nancy documents that there were few printers in town, and that the infrastructure for the print business scarcely existed.

By the time that Callot returned to Nancy Bellange had been dead for four years. Although we are here looking forward into the future, it is worth asking quite how the dukes used Callot in the twelve years until his death at the age of forty-two in 1635. For this might give some insight into the types of work in printmaking that were potentially available in Nancy, and thus how Bellange might have been employed. The surprising answer is that the dukes had very little use for Callot, despite the considerable financial inducements they made to encourage him to remain in Lorraine; similar inducements were given to the painters Claude Deruet and Jean Le Clerc.[53] The first job he was given in 1624 was to etch plates showing all the coinage that was legal tender in Lorraine. This was no doubt of great financial importance but hardly of great artistic interest. After this he was not given a single further ducal commission so far as we can tell. It is symptomatic that Callot never made a portrait of Charles IV. Between 1626 and 1630 he made three great six-plate views of sieges on commissions that came from outside Lorraine, two being from the King of France. Other works he had to make at his own expense and risk. That this was unsatisfactory may be deduced from the fact that from 1629 he regularly borrowed large sums from his old Nancy friend Israel Henriet, now settled in Paris as a dealer and publisher in prints. He repaid these debts by supplying Henriet with plates, so that in effect almost all the production of the last five years of his life was made for Paris, even though he was actually working in Nancy.

A few jobs did come to him locally, from other members of the court or from Catholic bodies such as the Jesuits. The most interesting of these was the so-called *Grand thèse*, made on a vast sheet of copper (615 × 519 mm) in 1625. It was commissioned for Nicolas-François (1609–70), the sixteen-year-old brother of Charles IV and at the time a student at the university of Pont-à-Mousson. Such theses listed the propositions that the student was to defend in a viva voce public examination, and gave its place and time. They were paid for by the student's family (this one was dedicated to his father), and their point was to create the maximum impression in order to launch the boy on a glittering career. In the case of Nicolas-François his family spared no expense. He was at the university between 1622 and 1629. In each of five of those years he published a thesis; in 1623 for rhetoric, in 1624 for logic, in 1625 for physics, in 1626 for general philosophy and in 1627 for theology. The first and fourth do not survive. The second was engraved by Jean Appier (Hanzelet) and dedicated to Duke Henri; the third was by Callot and dedicated to the boy's father; while for the fifth (dedicated to the Pope Urban VIII) the family went to Antwerp and to no less an engraver than Schelte a Bolswert, who had an international reputation as one of the leading collaborators of Rubens. The designer was Abraham van Diepenbeck (1596–1675), then at the beginning of his highly successful career.[54]

A small episode like this seems to epitomise neatly the paradox of the artistic patronage of small principalities. They could go to a local figure who might equally be a genius (Callot) or a hack (Hanzelet). Or they could go abroad, in which case their international connections led them to the right men: Bolswert, and to a lesser extent Diepenbeck, stood at the head of their professions. They were among the best available and doubtless cost a great deal to employ.

The Funeral of Charles III

On 14 May 1608 Charles III died after a reign of no less than sixty-three years. Since he took power on reaching his majority in 1559, he had raised the status and prosperity of his duchy to heights it had never reached before, and was never to reach again. It was seen as imperative that his funeral should be conducted with all possible ceremony. The body lay in state for weeks, and was finally buried two months later on 19 July. It was for Charles's body that the new circular funeral chapel was added onto the Church of the Cordeliers (see p. 16). At the beginning of 1609 Claude de la Ruelle, a court official who as councillor of state had been in charge of the ceremonies, published an unillustrated account of them under the title *Discours des Ceremonies, Honneurs et Pompe funèbre*.... It was dedicated to and written on the order of the new Duke Henri II. A year later, on 20 April 1610, another great ceremony took place when Henri II made his state entry into Lorraine on taking formal possession of the duchy. It seems to have been at this point that the decision was taken to have prints made of the principal scenes of both events. Only in this way would their full grandeur be conveyed to impress foreign courts. An exceptionally large edition of 1000 copies was made, and the prints distributed around Europe. A set in the British Library bears on the flyleaf a long contemporary dedication to Charles I when he was still Prince of Wales (that is before his accession to the throne in 1625) from someone signing himself *Ernestus princeps Germaniae*.[55]

The responsibility for having the plates made was again placed on Claude de la Ruelle. Fortunately both the prints and the contracts survive so we know a great deal about what happened.[56] Time was of importance and the plates had to be made quickly. This meant that they had to be etched rather than engraved. Friedrich Brentel (1580–1651), a printmaker from Strasbourg in Alsace, was brought to Nancy, and lodged and fed at La Ruelle's expense. He brought with him a copper-plate printer, Herman de Loye, as well as a boy, presumably Matthaeus Merian (1593–1650), who signed many of the plates. He was then only in his teens, and at the very beginning of what was to be a long and very distinguished career.[57] The contract had to be drawn up in both French and German as Brentel did not know any French; de Loye translated for him.

The contract envisaged two possibilities in the creation of the plates. The first were plates to be drawn by Brentel after six drawings of the same size which had been shown to him; for each of these he was to be paid 45 florins. The second were plates that were to be drawn on by 'the painters of Nancy'; for these Brentel was obliged to lay the grounds and apply the acid in biting them, and was to be paid half a florin. The reference to actual-size drawings is obscure, but the obvious guess is that they were by the court architect Jean La Hiere, who is credited with the 'perspectives' in the lettering of the plates[58]. The possibility that 'the painters of Nancy' might draw on the plates seems never to have happened. Brentel's surviving sketches (see later) prove that most of the figures that fill up the foregrounds in all the plates were of his devising.

A second contract drawn up two months later

between La Ruelle and de Loye covered the printing of the plates. One thousand copies of each plate were to be printed. For the smaller ones he was to be paid at the rate of 6 florins a thousand; the larger ones would cost twice as much. De Loye was to provide the ink, but La Ruelle provided the paper and paid for the copper. It was however de Loye who actually obtained the copper plates, according to the size of paper templates that La Ruelle had provided for each one. De Loye promised to ensure that the plates would be 'well beaten and polished', and the cost was fixed at half a florin per pound weight. One of the witnesses was Jean Callot, the father of Jacques.

The *Funeral of Charles III* is often discussed as if it is a book. It is implied that it is an example of the genre of what is now known as the 'festival' book, whose heyday was between the later sixteenth century and the end of the eighteenth century. These were series of plates designed to accompany a descriptive text, and took the form of a conventional book, with pagination and title-page. The *Funeral of Charles III* is nothing of the kind. Indeed were it not for the fact that the prints were commonly found laid down and bound between covers, it would not be described as a book at all. It consists in fact of five parts, with various groups of prints of quite different shapes and sizes, and the accompanying text comes on sheets of very varying size.[59] After the frontispiece the first ten plates show the lying-in-state and funeral of Charles III. The next forty-eight plates join together to show the long file of mourners in the funeral procession itself. A small advertisement says that the forty-eight prints can either be pasted together into the form of a roll or be mounted in strips of four to make 'a painting to hang in a room'; they could also be bound to accompany the text of the funeral (that is, the 1609 book) or simply be left in sheets. The third part contains another long procession, showing the entry of Henri II into Nancy in 1610 over twelve plates that join together. The fourth and fifth parts are quite different and much shorter, and serve as tail-pieces to what has gone before: four plates, dated May 1611, form another strip to show 'How Henri goes to church', while a large two-plate view of Nancy (fig. 4), also dated 1611, closes the ensemble.

If what is conventionally known as the *Funeral of Charles III* is one of the oddest 'books' of its time, it is also one of the most magnificent. Brentel was a fine artist, one of the best working in Germany at the time, and much of his large output still survives, including many preliminary drawings for the costumes of figures in this work that show the pains he took to get every detail right.[60] Many of the plates are exceptionally large, extending over two copper plates, and the grandeur of the undertaking and the detail of the scenes are quite exceptional. The allegorical frontispiece celebrates the achievements of Charles III and illustrates the words of his funeral oration, that the country owed to him the prosperity that had procured 'the introduction of diverse arts and of many beautiful commodities… unknown to his predecessors'. Among the small views of the riches of Lorraine is a scene representing *Opificina* (fig. 9), or 'manufacturing', surrounded by the tools of the various crafts that flourished in his reign. These include painting, sculpture, architecture and – just discernible – an engraving tool and a copper plate. Work on the book continued for at least a year from May 1610, and the effect in a small town such as Nancy,[61] which had never seen anything of the kind, must have been electric. Everyone would have known what was going on, and the artists in particular must have been fascinated.

Evidence that the most fascinated of them all was Jacques Bellange was only produced in 1971, when Nicole Walch, noting that one of the riders in the tenth

Fig. 9 Matthaeus Merian (1593–1650), *Opificina* (manufacturing), etching (detail from the frontispiece of the *Funeral of Charles III*). 97 × 83 mm. British Museum

plate of the procession of the entry of Henri II is etched in a completely different style from the others (no. 1), drew the conclusion that Bellange had etched it. And indeed the round eyes and slashed doublet of the rider and the ferocious expression of the prancing horse immediately announce the hand of Bellange himself. The label above the group states that these are the gentlemen of the *maison de son Altesse*, which is precisely what Bellange was. What is more likely than that, when Brentel came to this detail of the procession, Bellange decided that he would draw himself and told Brentel to leave him the space?

This plate would have been made late in 1610 or early in 1611, and to the accident of this commission we owe Bellange's introduction to the art of etching. He was probably in his later thirties, and all the other forty-seven plates we know from his hand must have been made in the following five years before his death late in 1616.

The Chronology of Bellange's Prints

Although we know when Bellange's first etching (no. 1) was made, only one of his other prints, the bookplate that he made for Melchior de la Vallée in 1613, is actually dated. An impression of no. 37 is inscribed in pen and ink with the plausible date 1614, while very early impressions of three prints (nos 9, 12 and 14) are printed on paper with a crowned H watermark which was only introduced in April 1613 (see pp. 126 and 130), so it can be reliably inferred that these prints were made after this date. Merian's copies of eleven of the prints may well have been made in 1615, although this hardly narrows down the possibilities. Otherwise a chronology can only be worked out stylistically or by an analysis of the signatures and inscriptions, but these are far from conclusive, and in any case a chronology loses its relevance when the prints were all made within such a short period.

The plates are inscribed in several different ways, two of which we can be certain are autograph signatures etched by Bellange. The first is the florid signature that combines the initial *J* with the *B*, used on *The Martyrdom of Saint Lucy* (no. 12), the set of the Three Magi (nos 29a–31a) and the *Hortulanae* (nos 32–5). In some instances the artist, inexperienced in etching letters (which is quite tricky as it has to be done in reverse), did not manage to fit in his whole name, so there are a variety of abbreviations within this group, and the *n* is reversed or elided with the *g*.[62] We know that in at least one instance this signature was etched before the plate was finished (see no. 32). A simplified variant of this signature appears on nos 4 and 5, which we might take to be earlier, whilst a more elaborate and accomplished variant appears on no. 13, which may be later. The second type of etched autograph signature is the neater cursive form used on two prints of the Virgin (nos 7 and 8a) and the two prints featuring hurdy-gurdy players (nos 36 and 37). This signature, which also combines the *J* and the *B*, is very similar to an example of Bellange's own handwriting on a document of 24 July 1616.[63] His inexperience in lettering is again evident in that the *ang* part of the signature is often reversed. Two examples of this signature are distinctly more crude than the rest, perhaps indicating an earlier date (see nos 6 and 10). As this signature was often added after the plate was finished, perhaps after a lapse of time (see no. 7), it must be used with caution as direct evidence for dating.

The inscriptions on the other plates are more of a problem, as some of them at least were added by a professional engraver. This is evidently the case with nos 39 and 40 which may well have received their inscriptions at the behest of a publisher rather than on the instruction of Bellange himself. The following pairs have the same type of lettering, perhaps engraved by the same person over a period of time: nos 11a and 38, nos 9 and 14 (rare first state impressions of which are printed on the same paper), and nos 15 and 16. Most of these include the title *Eques*, whereas only one of the autograph signatures cited above (on no. 13) includes the title. This might be taken as evidence that the majority of the plates with the autograph signatures are earlier, before Bellange was given the title, but, as the type of signature is different and as we do not know anything about when Bellange may have gained the title, this is very little help. Perhaps the most that can be said is that the stylistic evidence supports, rather than contradicts, the suggestion that these pairings with similar inscriptions each comprises two prints made around the same time, particularly in the case of nos 9 and 14, and nos 15 and 16.

A chronology based on the style and technique of the etchings has been worked out by previous writers, although they have disagreed as to where Bellange's style was heading when he died in 1616. As we know that all his etchings were made within five years it is more likely that the technical content of the prints will show development rather than the style *per se*. The sequence given by Worthen and Reed in 1975 pays particular attention to the technical development, and therefore seems more convincing to us than that given

by Thuillier in 1992, even though his analysis has been more recently accepted by Reed herself in 1994.[64] Thuillier describes Bellange progressing from an extreme Mannerism to a simpler, plainer figure style that prefigures the classicism introduced to Paris by Vouet in the 1620s. He therefore sees the more personal style of certain of the Apostles (no. 28) as earlier than those few that show a simpler, less mannered approach (no. 21a). Leaving aside the fact that the plainer appearance may be partly due to the plates being unfinished, this analysis seems questionable in the face of the evidence of Bellange's other prints. As Thuillier observes, the style and method of *The Holy Women at the Sepulchre* (no. 14), and even some of its poses and gestures, are close to certain of the Apostles (for instance, nos 22 and 28). But whereas Thuillier proposes that this is an early style, we see it as late because it is one of the most resolved and refined in terms of adapting the medium to Bellange's inventions.[65] For the same reason we would date the *Pietà* (no. 15) and *The Raising of Lazarus* (no. 16) as late and, like Walch, we would place these later than the group of three large multi-figure prints (nos 10–12), which are much fussier in terms of composition and decorative detail of costume and ornament. If this 'later style' is to be related to post-Mannerist stylistic currents, it is more likely a response to the painting of the Annunciation by Caravaggio that Henri II gave to the primatial church in Nancy, probably by 1610, and that evidently influenced Bellange's print of *The Annunciation* (no. 9).[66]

Thuillier also raises a new idea in proposing that many of Bellange's prints depend on paintings made some years earlier. Previous to this it had been assumed that the prints were independent works of art, partly because they lack the inscription *pinxit* usually found on prints reproducing paintings, but also because of the nature of the prints themselves. There is no real argument to support Thuillier's idea, which arises partly from his hypothetical stylistic chronology and partly from a reluctance to accept that Bellange would have gone to so much trouble to develop such complex and powerful compositions for any medium other than painting. A powerful argument against Thuillier's proposal is the number of extensive changes that Bellange made to the compositions during the etching process (see nos 11a and 15). He was clearly concerned with making etchings for their own sake, not with reproducing paintings. Although he may well have repeated figures and motifs from his paintings it is obvious merely from glancing through his prints that the reuse and re-invention of poses and gestures was a major constituent of his art. Unfortunately, Thuillier's assumption that the etchings reflect compositional ideas from an earlier period in his career inevitably distorts his chronology of Bellange's prints.

A further trap is the casual assumption that Bellange would have approached different subjects in the same way. In *The Holy Women at the Sepulchre* (no. 14) it can be seen that the artist appears less interested in stippling and hatching for the sake of differentiating flesh from drapery, but we must not assume that prints such as those of the Three Magi are necessarily earlier (or later) simply because they *do* show an interest in the depiction of texture. The Magi share some of the characteristics of costume prints, and part of the *raison d'être* of such prints was to depict a variety of textures, so we might expect a different approach from that employed in the depiction of the mystery of Christ's Resurrection. Similarly in the prints of beggars we cannot necessarily expect the approach to figure style to be the same as that applied to depictions of holy women and saints.

Bellange's Subject Matter

Bellange's prints divide roughly into the following categories of subject matter: small prints featuring devotional images of the Holy Family and saints (nos 3–8a); large prints depicting narratives from scripture or holy legend (nos 10–12, 14 and 16); single figures of the Apostles from an unfinished set (nos 17–28), single figures forming a set of the Three Magi (nos 29a–31a), and single figures relating to a set of *Hortulanae*, or 'Gardeners' (nos 32–5); prints of hurdy-gurdy players (nos 36–7); and just three prints relating to secular history or mythology (nos 38–40).

We do not know enough about Bellange's work as a painter to assess how closely this range of subjects reflects the content of his painting, but it is clear enough that there are certain subjects missing from the prints. The scenes of *commedia dell'arte* reproduced in de Passe's prints (see figs 13–16, p. 37) would probably have disappeared from Bellange's repertoire of subjects by the time he made his own etchings, as the fashion for these troupes at the ducal court had faded after 1600.[67] It is no surprise to find that he is documented as painting scenes of heroines from Roman history, including Portia (see no. 40), or devotional subjects such as Saint Francis and Mary Magdalene, but, given the nature of his decorations for the duke, we might expect a greater preponderance of prints of subjects from classical

authors or from mythology. However, the most extraordinary omission is the absence of portraits among his prints. Not only did most printmakers of the period produce portraits, but any artist employed in a princely court was called on to paint them as a matter of course and Bellange's prowess in this field was praised in a sonnet in 1606.[68] One might, however, surmise something of Bellange's capability as a portrait artist from visages such as that of the man in no. 31a.

Indeed, although we know of Bellange principally as the duke's painter, there are only a few elements in the prints that can be related directly to secular court art and culture. It has been suggested that the *Hortulanae* may relate to a specific ballet or masque,[69] and we can also find a strong trace of Bellange's gifts as a decorator and designer for fêtes and ballets in the extraordinary headdresses and lavish costumes that feature in so many of his other prints.[70] The rich combinations of luxurious fabrics and precious metals described in the court accounts for the ballets no doubt reflected and benefited from the new factories of such 'de luxe' items – silk and velour, gold and silver fabrics and thread – that Charles III established in the Ville-Neuve in the 1590s.[71] Another element worth noting is the depiction of numerous figures in Turkish or oriental costume (besides the Magi and the turbaned figures in no. 10, note particularly Veronica's headdress in no. 11a, the figure on the left of no. 39 and the 'Persian' treatment of Saint Jude, no. 27). This reflects a widespread contemporary curiosity which combined a dreadful fascination with the Turks (stemming from the wars with the Ottoman Empire) and a more general interest in things oriental.[72] *Turqueries* appeared in many of the ballets performed at court. In the ballet in honour of Marguerite of Gonzaga in 1606, for which Bellange decorated the triumphal chariot and possibly had a hand in the design of the costumes, the pages were dressed *à la Turque*, and in 1614 the three court ballets included a *Ballet à la Turque*.[73] Knowledge about the habits and dress of the Middle East was available through returning pilgrims, through books illustrating costumes of exotic lands,[74] and in publications such as Henri de Beauvau's best-selling guide to the Holy Land, Cairo, Malta and Constantinople, *Relation journalière du voyage du Levant...*, first published at Toul in 1608 with the help of Duke Henri II.

What is most striking is the predominance of religious subjects and specifically of the Virgin as a devotional figure. Of the forty-four subjects in this exhibition, the set of Apostles accounts for sixteen, and of the remaining twenty-eight, the Virgin appears in thirteen of them. This is not surprising if Bellange wanted to reach a wide audience abroad, but it was also a subject with a vivid relevance to everyday life in Lorraine.

The traditional affection for cults of intercession, whereby Mary or various saints would intercede on behalf of the worshipper, was closely allied to the veneration of images of these figures at places of pilgrimage. The miraculous powers accorded to these images were legion. Crowds flocked to them to celebrate their faith, cure their illnesses and exorcise evil spirits. Rather than try to vanquish these cults, the forces of the Counter-Reformation in Lorraine, principally the Jesuits at Pont-à-Mousson and the various monastic orders, especially the Franciscan convent of the Cordeliers in Nancy, tried to animate these popular beliefs with a more meditative spirituality based on their own teachings.[75] Mary was exalted in an abundant literature, both sophisticated and popular, and represented in art at all levels.[76] In 1606 the Jesuits created a Marial congre-gation called 'The Immaculate Conception' at the noviciate church in Nancy. The Chapelle Ronde was consecrated in 1612 to Notre-Dame-de-Lorette (Our Lady of Loreto). Loreto, the town in the Italian Marches where according to legend the house of Mary and Joseph in Nazareth (where the Annunciation took place) was transported by angels to save it from the Saracens during the Crusades, had become one of the main centres of pilgrimage besides Jerusalem, Rome and Compostela.[77] The son of Duke Charles III, Cardinal Charles de Lorraine, made a pilgrimage to Brabant to restore his health by praying to the Virgin of Montaigu. He brought back a wooden statue of the Virgin holding the infant Jesus and subsequently placed it, adorned with golden crowns, in the noviciate church, requesting that his heart be placed at the foot of the statue after his death.[78]

Other places of pilgrimage sprang up in Lorraine itself, including a chapel just outside one of the gates of Nancy, on the site of the victory of Duke René II in the battle of Nancy in 1477. René's victory was closely linked to the cult of Mary: the standard that he carried into battle bore an image of the Annunciation, and in thanks for her protection during the battle he commissioned a large sculptural group of the Annunciation for public display.[79] The chapel became known as Notre-Dame-de-Bonsecours because of the numerous miracles that took place there at the beginning of the seventeenth century, and many pilgrims came to venerate the statue of the Virgin placed within. The crowds became so great that in 1614 Duke Henri II

placed the pilgrimage in the care of the Order of Minims, who built a new church there.[80] This bustle of pilgrims provides a vivid context for Bellange's print of a hurdy-gurdy player attacking a pilgrim (no. 37); the badge of Saint James that the pilgrim wears had become a generalised badge of pilgrimage, so this figure may well be heading for Notre-Dame-de-Bonsecours.

Saints were venerated in a similar way. Fêtes and processions in honour of saints' days often included dramatisations of episodes from the saints' lives.[81] After 1600 there was a rash of biographies of saints, aimed at every level of society, which related colourful tales of the saints' ascetic and mystical exploits.[82] The biggest place of pilgrimage in Lorraine was the market town of Saint-Nicolas-de-Port where Saint Nicolas, who appears in one of Bellange's prints (see no. 2), was called upon to perform numerous miracles, reports of which increased after 1605.[83] The immediacy of the legends surrounding these figures is lost to us now, but it is worth bearing in mind how familiar Bellange's Apostle-Saints must have seemed to a contemporary audience, even if the appearance of many of them was unlike anything they had seen before.

Writers have often been tempted to relate the extraordinary depiction of spiritual figures in prints such as Bellange's *The Holy Women at the Sepulchre* (no. 14) with more esoteric Counter-Reformation theology or the poems of mystic writers such as Saint John of the Cross, but so far this has only been done in a vague way. The emphasis on the mannered outlines of the sweeping, tall-limbed figures within the darkened tomb – light against dark, dark against light – is not simply decorative, for it seems to be allied to an unnaturalistic use of light which in the context of the subject implies spiritual rather than natural sources. Unfortunately we have no way of knowing whether Bellange knew the theological texts that might give a more specific meaning to this use of light, but they were almost certainly available to him in Nancy, particularly the Italian and Spanish authors who were more widely read there than in Paris.[84] More important, we do not know whether Bellange intended that his figures should express these ideas nor whether contemporaries viewed them in this way. The most we can say is that the flame-like forms and luminous appearance of these figures within the darkened tomb, and also of some of the Apostles, have much in common with the descriptions and definitions of luminous spiritual light that penetrated theological discussion in Nancy around the time of Bellange's death.[85]

Bellange and the Art of Etching

When Bellange took his first steps on his own as an etcher he seems to have kept the technical process as simple as possible – no. 4, for instance, is etched with a single bite (immersion in the acid), with only a little retouching with a burin (engraving tool) to reinforce the contours. However, Bellange rapidly mastered the technicalities that produced the effects he admired in other prints, and the most complex of his prints display an extraordinarily subtle use of different processes.

The hatched shading in most of Bellange's prints was built up in layers. The artist would draw the first layer, then bite the plate in acid, then draw another layer, then bite the plate again, and so on. In the more sophisticated of the Apostles (nos 22 and 26) varnish has been painted on the plate to stop-out areas of shading halfway through the etching process; this produces the effect of the lighter 'shadow' down the left side of the figures. Most striking of Bellange's effects is the stippling of dots that he usually reserved for flesh (see no. 6) but were sometimes deployed for the lightest shading of drapery (no. 9). Some of these dots were etched, while others were added with a burin after the artist had finished etching the plate. The other tool that Bellange used in a very personal way was the burnisher, which was basically a polishing tool used to smooth the surface of the plate after the artist had scraped away some of the lines in order to make an alteration, such as we can see at the top of no. 24a. Bellange also made use of it to lighten areas and adjust the balance of shading within a print: if the lines of shading were polished down, they would hold less ink and therefore print a little lighter. The most spectacular example of this is the burnishing of Christ's face in no. 11a. Bellange also used the burnisher to polish the unetched areas of the plate when he wanted to make sure that the surface would trap no ink and therefore give him highlights that appeared as bright as the paper.

Few preparatory drawings survive for Bellange's etchings, and even those that have been put forward in some cases bear an uncertain relationship to the print. The most impressive case is the drawing in Yale University Art Gallery that was made preparatory to no. 4. This is executed in pen and brown ink with wash over black chalk on paper toned with ochre chalk; it is the same size as the print, and the outlines have been traced with a stylus for transfer to the plate (it is in reverse to the etching). Although certain modifications have been made (notably the omission of three angels in the background), the lines and hatched shading of the etching generally seem to be a direct recreation of the pen-lines and washed areas of tone in the drawing. Unfortunately, as this is probably one of Bellange's very early prints, and one that is still rather tentative in its use of the etching needle as distinct from the pen, this example cannot be taken as typical of Bellange's procedures in his later prints. The only other surviving drawing clearly connected with the whole composition of a print is one in Stockholm relating to no. 32.[86] This is in pen and wash, and includes an alteration to the position of the hand.

Bellange must have made compositional drawings for most of his other prints, especially as some of them are so ambitious and complex in their design. However, we can be sure that the process of compositional development continued once the plate was started. Various *pentimenti* appear on the prints, especially around the hands, which Bellange was so concerned to arrange in the most effective (sometimes it seems like the most contrived) of gestures. Most of the plates must have gone through many states, with Bellange printing off one or two proofs at each stage to see how work was progressing. Precious few of these survive (see nos 6, 7, 32 and 38). The proof of *Diana and the Hunter* in the Bibliothèque Nationale shows the earliest stage of work, with some passages, such as the faces, only sketched in outline, and with proposed additions drawn on the proof in chalk and ink. The proof from the Courtauld included in this exhibition (no. 6a), shows a plate taken to a further stage of resolution, with most of the areas that were to be shaded already showing stippling and hatching; these areas were slightly extended and substantially adjusted with burnishing and further work in the second state (no. 6b). The most obvious change, however, is the alteration of the position of the Virgin's hand, which is exactly what must have happened in many other instances where we do not possess working proofs (see no. 22b).

In most cases the surviving states differ only in whether they are signed or whether they bear a later publisher's name. An exception is the impression of the *Hortulana* (see no. 32) in Boston that bears the title but lacks some of the shading. In a few instances impressions that we can tell are very early from their richness and from the type of paper used bear the obvious traits of proofs taken by the artist: they are very inky, with smudges and fingerprints in the margin (see below under nos 8a and 12). The impression of *The Martyrdom of Saint Lucy* in the Prouté collection also lacks some of the burnishing seen in other impressions. But these instances are not so much exceptions as rare survivals.

In many other cases Bellange must also have added touches of burnishing and burin work at the last minute, but the proof impressions taken before these adjustments simply do not survive. Bellange would certainly have printed these proof impressions himself and would probably have used the back of the sheets for another proof or as a piece of scrap paper.[87] Later impressions, however, would have been made by a professional printer working either for Bellange or for a publisher.

The Production and Publishing of Bellange's Prints

We have already observed that the fact that twenty-two of Bellange's plates remained in his widow's possession after his death is very strong evidence that Bellange controlled the production of most of his prints. This conclusion is borne out by what evidence can be adduced from the study of the watermarks (see pp. 125–7). Not enough impressions have yet been properly examined to come to definitive conclusions. But there seems to be a pattern that the same watermarks are found on numbers of impressions of the same plate, thus suggesting that editions were run off by Bellange himself. Very early or proof impressions have different watermarks, as one would expect: these would be printed individually on odd pieces of paper found in the workshop, while editions would be printed on a pile of identical sheets bought in for the purpose. A few plates show aberrant patterns, most notably *The Death of Portia* (no. 40) and *Military Figures outside a City* (no. 39). They show four watermarks that are never found on any other Bellange print. Since these two plates are also connected in having a style of engraved lettering that is not found elsewhere, it seems reasonable to conclude that they were separated from the remainder and were printed differently – perhaps by being passed to a publisher.

A number of things follow from the fact that Bellange did control his own plates. First Bellange must have had access to a copper-plate press in Nancy. In 1610 the contract for the *Funeral of Charles III* specifies that Herman de Loye was to come from Strasbourg and bring his press with him. We can prove that there was an intaglio press in Nancy in 1615. In that year Jacob Garnich printed and published in Nancy a new illustrated edition of Henri de Beauvau's *Relation journalière du voyage du Levant*. The plates were made by Jean Appier the Elder and show two remarkable features: the first is that they were etched, not engraved, and the second is that the plates are printed on the same pages as the text. To do this Garnich must have had a copper-plate press to hand.

Appier and Bellange must also have had access to all the materials of print production in Nancy. It is difficult to believe that Bellange did his own printing; an artist of his stature had more profitable things to spend his time on. The most he would have done would have been to take proofs off incomplete plates. Once they were finished he must have employed his own printer, not necessarily full-time, but at least for weeks at a time to run off small editions. The capital to pay him and provide the paper must have come from Bellange himself.

How did he sell the impressions? The evidence for the existence of a print market in Nancy itself is tiny. Two mentions only have been found in the Nancy archives of printsellers: a Claude Liballe, *marchand de pourtraitz peintz et en taille douce* in 1609, and a Jean Marien, *marchand imagier demeurant a Nancy la neuve* in 1633.[88] He must have been able to sell his prints outside the town.

We here enter into areas of print history that have as yet hardly been explored. The one thing that is certain is that prints were distributed quickly, and that a distribution system did exist. Prints could be sold at one of many trade fairs of the day; prints often seem to have been sold at the same fairs as books. In Lorraine the main fair was that of Saint-Nicolas-de-Port, although there is no evidence as yet that prints were sold there.[89] The big publishers exchanged bundles of impressions, without cash changing hands. A recent study of the 1648 inventory of the heirs of Giuseppe I de' Rossi in Rome has calculated that 32 per cent of the individual sheets and 43 per cent of the books came from outside Rome.[90] It must also have been usual to sell impressions outright to a printseller or place them on consignment with him; he could then act as a wholesaler and sell them on. But evidence for this sort of trade is still lacking.

The proof of the efficacy of the distribution system is that innumerable prints were pirated across Europe within months of their production. Bellange himself suffered from such piracy, ironically at the hands of someone he must have known well. Matthaeus Merian, after the contract in Nancy had come to an end, had gone to Paris and then to Basle. While there he made a number of plates on contract for Jacob von der Heyden, a Netherlandish émigré who had settled in Strasbourg. Merian made copies of no less than eleven of Bellange's

Fig. 10 Matthaeus Merian (1593–1650), *Three Holy Women*, etching *c*.1615 (copy of Bellange no.13). 350 × 211 mm. Josefowitz collection

plates (fig. 10), and everything points to their having been made in 1615, which is within a few years or even months of their creation.[91] Strasbourg is close to Nancy, and was the closest large print-publishing centre. So it is no surprise that his etchings found their way there. He might even have been using von der Heyden as his distributor, only to find himself being cheated in this way.

If the publishing routes are unclear, we know even less about who the collectors were, since so little information survives about early seventeenth-century collecting. We do happen to know that the Englishman John Evelyn purchased an impression of Bellange's *Pietà* in Rome in 1645, for he wrote this information in the blank bottom margin of an impression that survives.[92] And the Roman collector Cassiano dal Pozzo had acquired an impression of Bellange's *Blind Hurdy-Gurdy Player* (no. 36) before his death in 1657.[93] How did these reach Rome? We can only guess that it may have been through the de' Rossi family, who we know had direct dealings with Parisian printsellers; in the desk of Domenico de' Rossi on his death in 1653 was a 'bundle of letters from Paris from François Langlois', the most important French dealer of his day.[94]

The Fate of Bellange's Plates after his Death

It is tempting to identify the twenty-two plates in Bellange's widow's possession in 1619 with those that were later sold to Le Blond, the Parisian publisher, who reissued eighteen of them with his own name added to the plate. Jean Le Blond (1590/94–1666) was a well-known and highly respected figure in Parisian publishing. In the dedications of some of his prints he describes himself as *peintre ordinaire du Roy*, but it is as a publisher that his name has survived. He published many of the early works of Abraham Bosse and, with Langlois and Pierre Mariette, took the lead in 1644 in presenting the case of the print trade against a government initiative that they thought would damage their interests.[95] This suggests that he was at the time one of the three leading dealers in Paris. His stock was very eclectic, spanning the entire range of production from pieces of great quality to ones aimed at a wide and general public taste.[96] The evidence of the watermarks suggests that all impressions from the eighteen plates with Le Blond's name are on exactly the same paper. In other words, Le Blond must have run off one very large edition, and then never reprinted the plates again. This implies that Bellange's work suddenly went out of fashion, and demand for it simply stopped.

What had happened to the remaining twenty-six plates that were not in his studio at his death? Some were the very small early plates that it is reasonable to think were experimental; the self-portrait in the procession of Henri II never belonged to him; and the Saint Norbert and the bookplate of Melchior de la Vallée must have been commissioned. The group of plates with Le Blond's 'address' includes none of the large plates. The evidence of their watermarks suggests that they had already been sold independently to other publishers, only one of whom put his name on the plate. This was van Merle, who put his name on the third state of *The Adoration of the Magi*. Van Merle was a minor figure, and his prints seem not to have been of any great quality. Since this plate unusually went on being published into the second half of the seventeenth century, it implies that he valued the plate more for its subject than for its author.

The largest group of missing items is the group of Christ and the Apostles. This is a very problematical ensemble, which is discussed more fully in the catalogue entries (nos 17–28). The surprising discovery that emerges from the study of the watermarks is that the Copenhagen set, as well as various individual impressions, are printed on the standard Le Blond paper, even though they do not carry his name. It is difficult to know what to make of this. Maybe other plates went to Le Blond, even though they do not have his name. Maybe there was a Le Blond edition before he added his name to the plates. This might explain why one type of grape watermark (wmk 2) is found fairly consistently on plates that later bore Le Blond's name, but not on anything else.

Bellange and Crispin de Passe

When Bellange etched his first plate, his self-portrait in the entry of Henri II in 1610/11, it was not his first experience of printmaking. He had already been involved with the business a decade earlier, in 1600 or 1601, when he supplied a number of drawings that were then engraved by Crispin de Passe. This obscure episode of his life needs closer examination.

Crispin de Passe was the founder of a great dynasty of engravers. He was born around 1565 and settled in Antwerp, which he was compelled to leave on account of his Protestant faith after it fell to the Spanish in 1585. In 1589 he was permitted to settle in Cologne, despite its being a Catholic town, where he remained until 1611. But in that year the town council became less tolerant,

INTRODUCTION

and he was forced to depart along with all his fellow Mennonites.[97] He then settled in Utrecht where he lived until his death in 1637. While in Cologne de Passe issued an abundant production of highly competent prints of subjects that could appeal to Catholic and Protestant alike. Most of them were after Marten de Vos's or his own designs; the eight he made after Bellange's are rather exceptional in his output. One of them, *The Three Holy Women at the Sepulchre* (fig. 11), forms part of a set of twenty oval scenes from the Passion made between 1600 and 1601; eighteen are after Crispin's own designs, and the exceptions are this and one other copied from a print after Federico Barocci. Another much larger plate of *The Adoration of the Magi* (fig. 12) is a single sheet, as is a smaller print of *The Beheading of Saint John the Baptist*. The remaining five prints and titleplate form a set of horizontal compositions with pairs of comic figures from the Italian comedy; the title is *Mimicarum aliquot facetiarum icones ad habitum italicum expressi* (of which four are reproduced as figs 13–16). One of these gives his name as designer.

Given that most of de Passe's plates are after his own designs, how are we to explain the fact that he made eight plates after Bellange, while no other engraver made any? Cologne is a long way from Nancy. The most obvious answer is that de Passe knew Bellange, that Bellange had visited him in Cologne and that he had stayed there while he made some drawings for him.[98] From the point of view of Bellange's later print production, such a hypothesis would help explain how he had acquired the knowledge and contacts, and thus the confidence, to embark on what was an extremely ambitious publishing programme on his own account a decade later.

Bellange's Origins and Style

This hypothesis has further implications. When looking at the documents on Bellange's life, we noted that he appears as it were from nowhere in 1602 with an appointment at court, and that the only earlier document comes from 1595 when he took on an apprentice

Fig. 11 (above right) Crispin de Passe (c.1565–1637) after Bellange, *The Three Holy Women at the Sepulchre*, engraving c.1600/1601. 138 × 107 mm (oval). British Museum

Fig. 12 (right) Crispin de Passe (c.1565–1637) after Bellange, *The Adoration of the Magi*, engraving c.1600/1601. 277 × 203 mm. Rijksmuseum

36

Figs 13–16 Crispin de Passe (c.1565–1637) after Bellange, four plates from *Mimicarum aliquot facetiarum icones…*, engravings c.1600/1601. Each c. 113 × 128 mm. Rijksmuseum (figs 13, 14, 15), British Museum (fig. 16)

at La Mothe. There is a gap of seven years that needs accounting for. There is also the important question of where Bellange got his artistic style from. His distinctive brilliance was all his own, but he had to start from somewhere.

There is plenty of evidence for links between the Upper Rhine and Nancy in the late sixteenth century. Specialists in mining were always welcome in Lorraine, and skilled German immigrants were being enticed

to populate the Ville-Neuve of Nancy.[99] If Bellange had been in Cologne and the southern Netherlands in all or some of the years between 1595 and 1602, much would fall into place. The contacts he had made and the fame he had gained from his association with de Passe would help explain how he got a prime job at the Nancy court so easily. The Netherlandish exposure also fits perfectly the style that is seen in his early designs for de Passe. By the time of his etchings in the 1610s he was a decade older and had time to develop a much more personal style. In 1600 he was still a young man and that much closer to his artistic exemplars. *The Adoration of the Magi* in particular reveals that those origins were Netherlandish Mannerism, as it emerged in the 1580s from the work of Bartholomeus Spranger.[100]

Karel van Mander, in his lives of Netherlandish artists, gives a famous account of the electric effect that the sight of Spranger's drawings had on Cornelis Cornelisz. and Hendrick Goltzius when he showed the drawings to them in Haarlem in 1583. Much Netherlandish art for several decades before this event can loosely be called Mannerist. Suddenly the way was open for a flowering of an extreme version of Mannerism that, depending on the taste of the viewer, can be regarded as wonderful and imaginative, or outlandish and ridiculous. For about thirty years from the 1580s this style had a remarkable success across Europe (fig. 17). Spranger himself worked at the court of Maximilian II in Vienna and of Rudolf II in Prague; another centre of Mannerism was the court in Munich; and Wendel Dietterlin (1550/51–99), an extraordinary figure whose *Architectura* is the most extreme application of Mannerist principles to architecture, had worked in Strasbourg, close to Nancy.

One very important aspect of this wave of Netherlandish Mannerism is that it was a style that lent itself admirably to printmaking, and inspired the production of a succession of masterpieces of the printmaker's art. These prints were all engravings rather than etchings. It was as a virtuoso engraver that Goltzius first made his international reputation, and around him grew a school of brilliant burinists (fig. 18). Their products were soon distributed around the world both by the network of publishers centred in Antwerp and by engravers who themselves travelled. The most celebrated family was the Sadelers. Of three brothers born in the Netherlands, Jan went to Frankfurt and Munich, and ended his life in Venice; Raphael settled in Munich; while Aegidius, the most famous of them all, went to Frankfurt and Italy, before ending his career as court engraver to Rudolf II in Prague. Seven members of the next generation of the family also entered the print business. Their prints went everywhere and can even be documented in Nancy.[101] Two engravings that Alexandre Vallée made in Nancy in 1592 were copied from prints after Spranger and Hans von Aachen.[102] A recently discovered thesis plate by Jean Appier Hanzelet dated 1618 is a copy from a well-known engraving by Jan Muller after Spranger made in 1604.[103] Bellange would certainly have known these prints; they were the sensation of the day, the masterpieces at the top of the market that everyone was talking about. And in Nancy Bellange would have realised that a reputation could be carried to the ends of the earth through the medium of prints far more than through paintings or drawings. This, as much as the profits to be made, must lie behind his intense application to the production of etchings.

But even if Bellange's style emerges from Netherlandish Mannerism, and his prints were inspired by the success and reputation of those by Spranger and his followers, there is still a missing element that needs to be explained in Bellange's artistic make-up. Even if his figures are recognisably cousins to those by Flemings, his way of drawing is utterly dissimilar. Goltzius and his school were line-engravers, who practised a virtuoso method of laying intersecting networks of swelling lines to give both volume and texture. Bellange was an etcher, and there is not a hint of a swelling line or the creation of volume by intersecting curves. His linear vocabulary is utterly different. He builds up his volumes and tones by laying one area of parallel lines over another; curved lines are only used to

Fig. 17 Aegidius Sadeler (*c.*1560–1629) after Bartholomeus Spranger, *The Three Holy Women Visiting the Tomb*, engraving 1600. 510 × 364 mm. British Museum

Fig. 18 Hendrick Goltzius (1558–1617) after Bartholomeus Spranger, *The Body of Christ Supported by an Angel*, engraving 1587. 328 × 251 mm. Fitzwilliam Museum, Cambridge

define the outer edges of shapes. For flesh, Bellange uses stippling, something that was very unusual, though far from unprecedented, in the history of etching.

The only precedents for all this are to be found in Italy, and in the work of two etchers in particular. The first is Federico Barocci, the second is his Sienese follower Ventura Salimbeni. An example of a Salimbeni and a Barocci are in this exhibition (nos 8b and 8c). Between about 1580 and 1585 Barocci (c.1535–1612) made four etchings, two small plates, and two large ones that were related to earlier paintings he had made.[104] The technical similarities with Bellange are striking. The volumes are created by overlaying areas of parallel lines; there is much stippling in the faces; and he used stopping-out varnish to step the depth of biting the lines, thus finding another way to achieve variations in tone.

The same devices can be found in the work of Ventura Salimbeni (1568–1613), who made seven etchings during a period which he spent in Rome, six

between 1589 and 1590 (see no. 8c), and one four years later in 1594.[105] Salimbeni is a far less famous artist than Barocci, and is a much less obvious name to associate with Bellange's. But this was an association that immediately occurred to Pierre-Jean Mariette, one of the greatest connoisseurs who ever lived. He never mentioned Barocci, but immediately thought of Salimbeni when discussing Bellange's *Virgin and Child with Cradle* (no. 6): 'In its method of engraving it is closely dependent on the manner of Ventura Salimbeni, and this might make one think that Bellange had studied under this master, or at least that he was trying to imitate him.'[106]

But there is no need to think that Bellange had ever gone to Italy. Salimbeni's prints were published in large numbers by a Roman publisher Cristoforo Stati; Barocci's must have been distributed equally widely to judge by the number of surviving impressions. So prints by both men would certainly have got to Nancy by 1610, a couple of decades after they had been etched. So the key to understanding the originality of Bellange's prints is to think of them as combining the compositions and figures of Northern Mannerism with the graphic language of Italian etching.

Bellange's Fame and Influence

One remarkable document suggests that Bellange's reputation was international. In 1620 Balthasar Gerbier wrote a memorial poem on Goltzius, who had died three years before. The relevant lines translate: 'Italy boasts of Raphael and Michelangelo, Germany of Albrecht Dürer, France of Bellange.'[107] Now Gerbier (1592–1667) was no idle versifier; he was one of the greatest experts on art of his day and a close friend of Rubens. Born in Middelburg in the Netherlands of émigré Huguenot parents, he came to England in 1615 and for eight years from 1620 was the agent who built up the extraordinary collection of paintings of the Duke of Buckingham; later he worked for other collectors, including Charles I.[108] So his view signifies a great deal, even though no other comparable statement from such an early date has yet been discovered.

The next document is thirty years later and is a passage from a poem, *La ville de Paris en vers burlesques* by Le Sieur Berthaud, first published in 1652. The narrator meets Guérineau, a vendor of drawings, who obligingly lists his stock: 'I have some fine works by Caravaggio, Titian and Carracci; I have pieces of Tintoretto, Parmigianino and Albrecht Dürer; I have the Danae of Farnese, two large drawings of Veronese, the architecture of Hondius, the nudes of Goltzius and four crayons made by Bellange, and three others by Michelangelo…'[109] Such a high valuation of Bellange's drawings is born out by the number of drawings by him, or in his manner, that have his name written on them by early owners. The very fact that many are not by him shows how his was the great name to which minor works automatically gravitated.[110] The fact that there are so many in his manner also show that his drawings must have been widely available and influential.

Yet his etchings had no such influence. No one else tried to make prints that even remotely imitate his manner. His former apprentice Claude Deruet made a handful of etchings, all now very rare. The grandest of them is an equestrian portrait of Duke Charles IV of Lorraine. An impression of the first state printed on silk is in the British Museum (fig. 19), and shows both a style and a manner of etching that has nothing to do with Bellange. Callot must have met Bellange before his departure for Italy. But again there is no trace of influence. Nor is there in the single etching by another artist from Lorraine, Georges Lallemand, who made his career in Paris. Lallemand holds a significant place in

the history of printmaking because of his collaboration in the 1620s with the German woodcutter Ludolph Büsinck in a series of twenty-three chiaroscuro woodcuts for which he supplied the drawings.[111] These are entirely *sui generis*, which is why they are so interesting, but the only link with Bellange is in certain aspects of their subject matter.

Yet we know that Bellange's prints were valued. Seventeenth-century writers on printmaking mention his name. The first is John Evelyn, whose *Sculptura* of 1662 goes back to years spent in Paris in the later 1640s. In it Bellange is only a name in a list,[112] but we have already mentioned that he owned an impression of his *Pietà* as well as the copy of it by Merian (p. 35). In 1675 the German historian Joachim von Sandrart praised his *besonders gute Manier*.[113] The great print collector, Michel de Marolles, noted his name several times. In the catalogue of his first collection in 1666, which was purchased by Louis XIV, he lists in volume 78 an *oeuvre* of Bruegel and Bosch in 116 pieces and of *le cavalier Jacques Bellange* who made forty-seven prints with his own hand – a total of 163 prints. In the catalogue of his second collection, published in 1672, he had forty-nine prints by Bellange bound up in the same album as numerous prints after Philippe de Champaigne, 635 by

Fig. 19
Claude Deruet
(*c*.1588–1660),
Charles IV of Lorraine,
etching 1628,
printed on silk.
342 × 472 mm.
British Museum

Fig. 20 Matthaeus Merian
(1593–1650), Four *Hortulanae*,
etchings *c*.1616, copied from
Bellange nos 32–5, as mounted
for Cassiano dal Pozzo.
449 × 260 mm (overall).
British Library

François Chauveau, and others of very assorted types – a total of 824 prints.[114] Bellange is also mentioned three times, though more as a draughtsman than an etcher, in Marolles's *Livre des Peintres et Graveurs* of *c.*1677.[115] Perhaps the most significant point that emerges from these catalogues are the numbers of forty-seven and forty-nine: we now think that Bellange made forty-eight prints, so virtually all the prints by Bellange that we know today were already known then.

The popularity of his prints is supported by the fact that most of his etchings survive in significant numbers; most of the major print cabinets hold a respectable group of his prints, and in 1785 the English connoisseur Joseph Strutt only bothered to list four of Bellange's prints in his dictionary 'because his works are by no means uncommon'.[116] For so many to survive, they must have been sold in large numbers at the time and have been well looked after in collections. Von der Heyden in Strasbourg thought it worth getting Merian to copy no less than eleven of them in 1615/16 – one of the most concentrated bursts of piracy of the period. These copies had stated that Bellange was the designer, and they helped spread knowledge of his work. The collection assembled by Cassiano dal Pozzo in Rome before his death in 1657 contains a mixture of Bellange's originals and Merian's copies (fig. 20).[117] We must remember too that after Bellange's death, his etched plates were regarded as valuable property and were sold to Le Blond, a leading Parisian publisher, who printed a large edition of them.

Bellange's Reputation since the Seventeenth Century

Unfortunately Bellange found no biographer. There was no Vasari or van Mander to write in French on art before the second half of the seventeenth century. By the time that Félibien wrote his *Entretiens* at the end of the century the facts about Bellange and most of his contemporaries had been forgotten. He only mentions Bellange as a pupil of Vouet; if true at all, this can only refer to his son Henri.[118] Mariette, in the eighteenth century, had only heard echoes of a forgotten reputation: 'he had his admirers, and Bellange had a great vogue'.[119]

What was fatal to Bellange's later reputation was the stylistic revolution that hit French painting in the late 1620s. Later critics placed the rise of the French school precisely in 1627, the year that Vouet returned to Paris from Italy. Vouet was not only extremely successful

himself, but he took on a stream of immensely talented students. These were in turn to become the leading lights of French painting and the founders of the Académie Royale de Peinture in 1648. From that point the course of historiography was fixed, and Bellange played no part in it.

But the existence of the large body of his etchings, all bearing his name, meant that he was never completely forgotten. Hence he found his way into the notes of Mariette, and other eighteenth-century sources. But Mariette was uncertain about his real name. Père Husson, writing in 1766,[120] had stated that his first name was Thierry; Mariette could see that this was wrong from the initial on the plates, but he read this as a capital G. Marolles had called him Jacques; was the G for Giacomo, the Italian version of Jacques?

All these perplexities were ended when the archivists of the mid-nineteenth century discovered the documents that began to reveal the man himself and his career. These historians, with Henri Lepage at their head, were local Lorraine patriots, and for them any native figure took on a heroic cast. Outside Lorraine he was still ignored. Robert-Dumesnil, whose scholarly conscientiousness forced him to include Bellange's prints in *Le Peintre-Graveur Français* in 1841, quoted a disparaging comment by Mariette's successor, Basan, from 1767:[121] 'a bad painter, and even worse engraver of the last century…he has etched several pieces of his own composition, where there is much more bizarreness than judgement and very little correctness.' Robert-Dumesnil went on to claim indulgence for a few of the Madonnas, which he thought charming, but agreed that the rest was detestable: his compositions were bizarre and utterly incorrect, so much so that if Bellange was alive in 1841 he would merit a place as ringleader of the romantic school, whose methods and power he had stumbled on two centuries in advance.[122]

Later authorities simply ignored him. This neglect lasted extraordinarily late. Between 1923 and 1929 François Courboin, the director of the Cabinet des Estampes in the Bibliothèque Nationale, published a massive standard work, his *Histoire Illustré de la Gravure en France*;[123] Bellange is not mentioned. In A. M. Hind's standard English-language *History of Engraving and Etching*, first published in 1908 and revised in 1911 and 1923, his name only appears in a list of engravers at the end. The comparable standard work in German was Paul Kristeller's *Kupferstich und Holzschnitt in vier Jahrhunderten*, first published in 1905 and in a fourth edition in 1922. Bellange is indeed mentioned in two sentences but only to be dismissed by comparison with his fellow-countryman Callot: 'But he fell in the mannerisms of Salimbeni's distortions of form, from which Callot was quickly saved by his healthy nature.'[124]

Bellange's escape from the ghetto of the local antiquarian and the print specialist was part of the wider re-evaluation of Mannerist art, which Mariette had confidently thought would never take place: 'It appears that he tried to imitate the manner of Spranger, which was itself at the time regarded as the only one that ought to be followed. Happily people soon turned away from it, and it will never rise again.' Today this reads rather like Dr Johnson's famous verdict on Laurence Sterne: 'Nothing odd will do long. *Tristram Shandy* did not last.'

The first article that reintroduced Bellange to a general public was by Ludwig Burchard in 1911. Burchard came from Mainz, and his study of Bellange was a spin-off of his pioneering work on Dutch etchers before Rembrandt. His article was published not in a specialist art-historical journal but in a general art magazine, *Kunst und Künstler*.[125] Burchard was judiciously cautious about the claims he made for Bellange, and his article was probably read by few. The effective rediscoverer of Bellange for the twentieth century was the great Viennese art historian Max Dvořák in one of his most influential lectures, published after his death in 1921. 'Über Greco und den Manierismus'[126] succeeded in reawakening enthusiasm for the entire period of Mannerism by reinterpreting it in positive terms as the expression of the religious sensibility of the years of the Counter-Reformation. The four artists illustrated in his article were El Greco, Michelangelo, Tintoretto and Bellange.

It was no accident that this happened in Vienna, immediately after the First World War. These were the years of the triumph of Expressionism and of Freud. Dvořák had witnessed the success of Kokoschka and Schiele. It was Kokoschka who painted a famous double-portrait of Hans and Erica Tietze-Conrat in 1909 (now in the Museum of Modern Art, New York), and it was Erica who took Dvořák's argument further in her monograph, *Der Französische Kupferstich der Renaissance*, in 1925. Her text is full of Freudian language, and her interpretation of Bellange is still startling: 'The way in which the artist sees forms is strongly sexual, perversely sexual; and entirely genuine, since it mirrors the artist's sub-conscious. Otherwise he would never have drawn Saint John in a series of Apostles in so female a fashion…the angel of the Annunciation is a hermaphrodite, but not with mixed

but with marked characteristics of either sex….' This kind of interpretation has been remarkably influential. At its most extreme it has led to the absurd but often voiced thought that Bellange must have been homosexual.[127]

The main strain of writing has, however, depended more on Dvořák than Freud. This reached the English-speaking world through another Viennese, Otto Benesch, a pupil of Dvořák and the son of one of Egon Schiele's first patrons (father and son are the subject of a double-portrait in 1913, now in the museum at Linz). His book, *The Art of the Renaissance in Northern Europe: Its Relation to the Contemporary Spiritual and Intellectual Movements*, was first delivered as a series of lectures when an emigré in Boston in 1944. His introduction to Bellange is worth quoting in full:

The Gothic trend in French Renaissance art increased in the second half of the sixteenth century and finally reached its climax around 1600. The more the serenity of spirit which dominated the era of Francis I was replaced by a serious, contemplative, mournful mood, the general mood of the Western world in the era of the Counter Reformation, the more the shadows of the Middle Ages raised their gigantic heads. The body is a prison from which the soul longs to be freed. The enjoyment of physical beauty and nature recedes. If the forms transcend nature, it is not in order to obey a canon of beauty, but to convey expression of soul, depth of sentiment. The light which illuminates the way of men is not sun and moon shining on bosquets with nymphs and fauns, but the light of religion, of faith, of the beyond, the light which shines with a supernatural glare at the end of the long dark tunnel of earthly life. This feeling found its strongest expression in France in the sculptures of Germain Pilon, in the etchings and drawings of Jacques Bellange, and in the writings of Saint François de Sales.[128]

Such has been the power of this type of interpretation that it surfaces almost unconsciously in authors who are far removed from this intellectual tradition. Even though he includes neither author in his bibliography, it is by Dvořák and Benesch that Anthony Blunt was influenced when he wrote in 1953: 'The etchings of Jacques Bellange are the last in a long evolution of that particular type of Mannerism in which a private mystical form of religious emotion is expressed in terms which appear at first sight to be merely those of empty aristocratic elegance.'[129] Since Blunt goes on to provide the best analysis of Bellange's compositional devices yet written, it is not surprising that the influence of this interpretation has continued. It still lingers, for example, in John Shearman's book, *Mannerism*, of 1967, where Bellange is coupled with El Greco as two artists who 'used strongly Mannerist conventions with an increasingly expressive purpose and urgency that is far from characteristic of Mannerism'.[130] The problem here is to distinguish what is personal from what was the style of the age. The age was indeed one of intense spirituality and Nancy was a home to it (see pp. 30–31). But there is no reason to think that Bellange's feelings and beliefs in any way stood apart from those of his contemporaries.

The credit for using the Nancy archives to put Bellange firmly back into his place and time belongs unquestionably to F.-G. Pariset in the long series of articles he published between 1929 and 1965 on all aspects of Bellange's work, although he never produced the monograph he promised. He has been followed by such excellent historians in Nancy as Pierre Marot and Paulette Choné.

Meanwhile the appreciation of Bellange in the wider world of art and print historians has grown apace. It was, perhaps inevitably, in Vienna, in the Albertina, that the first exhibition ever devoted to Bellange took place in 1931 or 1932.[131] The first American writer was H. P. Rossiter in the Boston Museum Bulletin of 1942, and it was Rossiter who built up the great collection in the Museum of Fine Art, Boston, that lay behind the second Bellange exhibition, and the first with a catalogue, mounted by Amy N. Worthen and Sue Welsh Reed in 1975.[132] It was this exhibition that provided the stimulus for the creation of the private collection catalogued here.

Bellange has now become an artist whose towering presence forces his inclusion in any collection. An artist-collector such as Georg Baselitz has included no less than seven Bellange's in his choice group of 103 Mannerist prints.[133] But scholars continue to feel uncomfortable in finding the right art-historical slot in which to confine him. In 1967 Konrad Oberhuber put on an exhibition in the Albertina with the title, *Zwischen Renaissance und Baroque: das Zeitalter von Bruegel und Bellange*. Here he stands at the beginning of the Baroque. More recently a Franco-American team including Cynthia Burlingham, Marianne Grivel and Henri Zerner has put on an exhibition of prints from the Bibliothèque Nationale with the title, *The French Renaissance in Prints*.[134] This began around 1500 and ended with Bellange; here Bellange is presented as a Renaissance artist, and neither Mannerist nor proto-Baroque. The present exhibition is the first devoted to his work to be shown in Britain, Holland and Denmark. Never since the 1620s has Bellange been so highly valued, though he is still insufficiently known to a general public.

Notes

Principal sources are abbreviated as follows (in chronological order):

Lepage 1854: Henri Lepage, 'Quelques notes sur des peintres Lorrains', *Bulletin de la Société d'Archéologie Lorraine*, IV 1854, pp. 5–79.

Roy 1913: Hippolyte Roy, 'La vie à la cour de Lorraine sous le duc Henri II', *Mémoires de la Société d'Archéologie Lorraine*, LXIII 1913, pp. 53–206 (and separately printed)

Walch 1971: Nicole Walch, *Die Radierungen des Jacques Bellange: Chronologie und kritischer Katalog*, Munich 1971

Worthen–Reed 1975: Amy N. Worthen and Sue Welsh Reed, *The Etchings of Jacques Bellange*, exhibition catalogue, Des Moines Art Center, Iowa 1975

Sylvestre 1981: Michel Sylvestre, 'Jacques-Charles de Bellange, *gentilhomme suivant son Altesse*, peintre et graveur', *Le Pays Lorrain*, 1981 no. 4, pp. 207–28.

Choné 1990: Paulette Choné, 'Jacques Bellange et son fils Henri: nouveaux documents', *Le Pays Lorrain*, vol. 71 1990, pp. 71–90.

Choné 1991: *Emblèmes et Pensée Symbolique en Lorraine (1525–1633)*, Paris 1991

Nancy 1992: *L'Art en Lorraine au temps de Jacques Callot*, exhibition catalogue Musée des Beaux-Arts, Nancy, 1992. The entries on Bellange are by Jacques Thuillier, and most of the documents concerning Bellange are reprinted on pp. 382–8.

The most up-to-date summary of Bellange's life and work is in the entry on him contributed by Paulette Choné to the new *Saur Künstler-Lexikon*, VIII 1994, pp. 434–7. It contains a very full bibliography.

1 The only published attempt is the list of 53 drawings in the entry by P. Choné on Bellange in the new *Saur Künstler-Lexikon*, VIII 1994, pp. 435–6. There is also a catalogue with 94 paintings and drawings in C. D. Comer, *Studies in Lorraine Art c.1580–c.1625*, PhD. Princeton University 1980.

2 Pierre Rosenberg identified the hand of Jean de Saint-Igny in the *Burlington Magazine*, CXXIV 1982, pp. 694–7; another artist whose drawings are often confused with Bellange's is Georges Lallemand.

3 The latter two paintings are reproduced as nos 4 and 6 in the 1992 Nancy exhibition catalogue, *L'Art en Lorraine au temps de Jacques Callot*, which gives further references. The pair of the Annunciation is reproduced as plate 1 of the 1959 exhibition *Das 17te Jahrhundert in der französischen Malerei* at the Kunstmuseum Bern.

4 Choné 1990, p. 72.

5 For this section see C. Pfister, *Histoire de Nancy*, 3 vols, Nancy 1902–9; G. Ciotta, 'La fondazione della Villa-Nuova di Nancy ad opera di Carlo III' in *Quaderni del Istituto di Storia dell'Architettura*, 1977–8, pp. 49–68; P. Choné in *Le Grand Nancy*, Nancy 1993; and B. Heckel in *Jacques Callot*, exhibition catalogue, Nancy 1992.

6 Georges Aulbéry, *Histoire de la vie de St Sigisbert… comprenant plusieurs singularitez du duché et de la ville de Nancy*, Nancy (Jacob Garnich) 1617, quoted by Choné 1991, pp. 218–19.

7 Choné 1991, p. 231.

8 Choné 1991, p. 238.

9 P. Choné, 'Le Prince, le jardin, la science', *Le Pays Lorrain*, 1993 pp. 147–52.

10 L. Châtellier, 'La vie religieuse à Nancy', in *Actes du colloque Jacques Callot 25–7 Juin 1992*, Paris 1993, p. 166; and Choné 1991, pp. 208–9.

11 A set of early copies of these paintings was discovered in the public library of St Petersburg and published by Nicole Reynaud in *Revue de l'Art*, 61 1983, pp. 7–28. J. Guillaume, 'La Galerie des Cerfs de Nancy', *Revue de l'Art*, 75 1987, p. 44, reproduces a drawing of *c.*1700 which shows the combined deer and roundels.

12 See Hippolyte Roy, *La vie, la mode et le costume au XVIIe siècle, étude sur la cour de Lorraine*, Paris 1924, p. xiii.

13 The principal source from which the following is derived is Lepage 1854.

14 Deruet was paid 150 francs for the bedposts in 1624. See M. E. Meaume, 'Recherches sur la vie et les oeuvres de Claude Deruet', *Bulletin de la Société d'Archéologie Lorraine*, IV 1854, p. 152. In 1595–6 Claude Henriet painted the names of the streets in the Ville-Neuve on 72 iron plaques, to be stuck onto the walls. See H. Lepage, *Les Archives de Nancy*, Nancy 1865, II p. 193.

15 C. D. Comer, 'Three drawings by Médard Chuppin', *Master Drawings*, XXII 1984, pp. 298–303. Two more unsigned drawings of the same type have since been discovered: see E. Brugerolles, *Le dessin en France au XVIe siècle; Dessins et miniatures des collections de l'Ecole des Beaux-Arts*, exhibition catalogue, Paris 1994, pp. 244–7. Cf. P. Choné, 'Le dessin d'une fête masquée à la cour de Lorraine (février 1580)', in *Chloé, Beihefte zum Daphnis*, XV 1993, pp. 377–404.

16 See Ian Wardropper, 'Le mécénat des Guise; art, réligion et politique au milieu du XVIe siècle', *Revue de l'Art*, 94 1991, pp. 27–44.

17 See Choné 1991, p. 245.

18 Choné 1991, pp. 240–52.

19 The whole poem is quoted in the original French by Worthen–Reed 1975, p. 14.

20 This unpublished letter was found by Brigitte Heckel; we owe our knowledge of it to Paulette Choné.

21 See, for example, Roy 1913, pp. 145 and 150.

22 A. Jacquot, 'Notes sur Claude Deruet', *Réunion des Sociétés des Beaux-Arts des Départements*, XVIII 1894, publishes the inventory of Deruet's estate in 1660. This contained a number of paintings by Bellange.

23 See note 11.

24 H. Lepage, 'Le Palais Ducal de Nancy, I Galerie des Cerfs', *Bulletin de la Société d'Archéologie Lorraine*, I 1851, pp. 112–14.

25 F-G. Pariset, 'Le mariage d'Henri de Lorraine et de Marguerite Gonzague-Mantoue; les fêtes et le témoinage de Jacques de Bellange', in *Les Fêtes de la Renaissance*, Paris 1956, pp. 153–89. See Choné 1991, p. 190, for details of the carriage.

26 See *The King's Arcadia: Inigo Jones and the Stuart Court*, exhibition catalogue, Banqueting House, Whitehall, 1973, p. 36.

27 Félibien's statement (*Entretiens sur les Vies et sur les Ouvrages des plus excellens peintres*, 2nd edn Paris 1696, II p. 189) that Bellange was an employee of Vouet, which caused great confusion among early writers, probably refers to the son, who may well have been one of the numerous painters who worked for a time in Vouet's studio. Henri's work is very little known, though a thesis on his drawings by Christophe Georgel was presented to the University of Dijon in 1994 (information from P. Choné). There exist two undated sets of prints after his designs: twenty plates of acrobats, and ten of characters of the *commedia dell'arte*. Both were issued by an unrecorded publisher Rocher with an address 'sur le quay de l'Orloge' (a copy is in the British Museum).

28 Published Choné 1990, pp. 84–6. Choné has added further information in her entry on Henri in the *Saur Künstler-Lexikon*, VIII 1994, pp. 432–3.

29 Deruet was created a *Cavaliere di Portugal* by Pope Paul V in 1619 and used this title on his return to Nancy the following year. In 1621 he was given letters of nobility in Lorrain. Callot inherited his nobility from his grandfather Claude, who had been raised to it in 1584.

30 Choné 1990, p. 71.

31 Sylvestre 1981, p. 217.

32 See Lepage 1854, pp. 49–51.

33 This was put forward by Choné 1990, p. 74.

34 Published by Sylvestre 1981, p. 227.

35 Paulette Choné suggests to us that this might have been a gambling debt; the duke regularly lost and won huge sums.

36 The original text reads: 'non compris toutesfois en ce present obligatoire…le pris de vingt deux pieces de lames de cuivre figurées en plusieurs sortes d'histoires, quy ne scauroient pheu appréciée par peintres, pour n'estre de leur congnoissance, ains d'espertz imprimeurs…' See Sylvestre 1981, p. 227.

37 Domenico Tempesti, *I Discorsi sopra l'intaglio*, edited by Furio de Denaro, Florence 1994, p. 144.

38 Vittorio Zonca, *Novo Teatro di machine et edificii*, Padua 1621, pp. 76–8 (1st edn 1607). This book, although mentioned by Hind and other early writers, has not been referred to in recent literature. We owe our knowledge of it to David Woodward, who discussed it in his 1995 Panizzi lectures at the British Library on sixteenth-century Italian maps and prints (to be published late in 1996).

39 See Annette Manick, 'A note on printing inks' in Sue Welsh Reed and Richard Wallace, *Italian Etchers of the Renaissance and Baroque*, Boston 1989, pp. xliv–xlvii.

40 See M. Bimbenet-Privat and F. Le Bars, 'New documents on XVIth century printmaking in Paris', *Print Quarterly*, XI 1994, pp. 151–5.

41 A complicating possibility, to which Zonca makes no reference, is to re-etch the plate to strengthen the lines. This trick involves the careful laying of a new ground without filling up the etched lines. It was certainly practised by the eighteenth century, but when it was first introduced is unknown.

42 For Woeiriot's biography, see Choné 1991, pp. 543–68. For his prints, see A.-P.-F. Robert-Dumesnil, *Le Peintre-Graveur Français*, VII 1844, pp. 42–140. Woeiriot's son Pompée was paid

an annual wage by the duke from 1593 until his death in 1617 as his 'peintre illumineur'. Bellange must have known him and his father's work.

43 Albert Kolb, 'Die Anfänge der Druckkunst in Nancy', *Gutenberg-Jahrbuch* 1930, pp. 209–25.

44 For Vallée, see Choné 1991, pp. 405–6. His prints are in Robert-Dumesnil, op. cit., VIII and XI.

45 For Appier, see Nancy 1992, p. 378, and the *Inventaire* of the Bibliothèque Nationale. We are also indebted to information from Paulette Choné.

46 See the documents in Nancy 1992, pp. 378–82, and the *Inventaire* of the Bibliothèque Nationale.

47 H. Lepage, *Les Archives de Nancy*, Nancy 1865, II p. 219.

48 The standard works on Callot are the works by Lieure and Marot referred to in the following notes. See also the recent catalogue of an exhibition, *Jacques Callot 1592–1635*, held at the Musée Historique Lorrain in Nancy in 1992.

49 See J. Lieure, *Jacques Callot, la vie artistique*, Paris 1929, part II pp. 17–18.

50 This happened before 1627, the year in which Lucini made a set of 24 plates of Gobbi in a Callot-like manner. The titleplate reads: 'Compendio dell Armide cara mogi d'Ant. Fran. Lucini. In Firenze MDCXXVII'. The publisher, most surprisingly and interestingly, was F. L. D. Ciartres (i.e. Langlois) in Paris. A complete set is in the Bibliothèque Nationale, Tf 1, pp. 97–8.

51 See P. Marot, 'Jacques Callot, sa vie, son travail, ses éditions, nouvelles recherches', *Gazette des Beaux-Arts*, LXXXV 1975, p. 24.

52 See L. H. Wüthrich, *Das druckgraphische Werk von Matthäus Merian d. Ä.*, I, Basel 1966, p. 75 and elsewhere.

53 See documents in the 1992 Nancy exhibition catalogue.

54 See J. Favier, 'Les thèses du Prince Nicolas-François de Lorraine', *Mémoires de la Société d'Archéologie Lorraine*, LXII 1912, pp. 75–98. Choné 1991, p. 731, n. 32, has published some interesting documents concerning one of these theses: the paper came from Toul and was of an exceptional size for which new moulds had to be made; three copper plates were ordered from Jean Mellin (brother of the painter Charles Mellin) at the Nancy copper mill, while a marble mason polished them before engraving.

55 Pressmark 651 a.2. The identity of Ernestus is unclear; all that can be said is that as a prince he was a member of a royal house but not actually a ruler himself (information from Peter Barber).

56 See P. Marot, 'Contrats passés pour la gravure et l'impression des planches de la Pompe Funèbre de Charles III, duc de Lorraine', *Gutenberg-Jahrbuch*, 1951, pp. 140–45. Marot had previously published an excellent monograph, *Recherches sur les pompes funèbres des ducs de Lorraine*, Nancy 1935.

57 Despite his youth, Merian had completed his apprenticeship and had already signed and dated a plate in 1609. It was presumably for this reason that he was allowed to sign some of the prints in Nancy. But it is then odd that he is referred to as a 'boy'.

58 The lettering presents various other points of interest to a print historian. It states 'Claude de la Ruelle inventor', which cannot mean that he drew the design (as it would normally signify), but rather that the whole event was of his devising. 'Herman de Loye excudit' likewise cannot have its normal meaning that he published it; the documents show that La Ruelle was the publisher, while de Loye was simply the printer. An important study 'Nicolas et Jean La Hiere, architectes des ducs de Lorraine 1589–1611' was published by Jacques Choux in *Lotharingia*, III 1991, pp. 5–122.

59 The letterpress is by Blaise André, the ducal printer. On the sheets where there was so much text that a smaller type had had to be used to fit it in, André's name is replaced by 'Nancei, Typis Jacobi Garnich'. Evidently he had to borrow Garnich's type, or subcontract these sheets to him, as he himself had no font small enough.

60 On Brentel see Heinrich Geissler, *Zeichnung in Deutschland 1540–1640*, Stuttgart 1980, II pp. 36–8; and Wolfgang Wegner, 'Untersuchungen zu Friedrich Brentel', *Jahrbuch der Staatlichen Kunstsammlungen in Baden-Württemberg*, III 1966, pp. 107–96, with a catalogue of his prints that improves on Andresen and Hollstein.

61 A small example of this point: the Callot family lived at 33 Grand Rue. Two doors away, at no. 31, was the goldsmith Humbert de la Vallée. His son Melchior, a priest who figures prominently in Duke Charles's funeral procession as does Callot's father, was the man for whom Bellange etched a bookplate. Bellange also acted as witness at the wedding on 23 March 1609 of Melchior's sister Françoise. Her husband was a certain Jean de Saint Paul, a painter from Neufchâteau then living in Nancy. Jean's brother or nephew Antoine is recorded working for Bellange's partner Danglus in 1605.

62 There is also little consistency as to whether *f.*, or *fec.*, or *fecit*, or nothing at all was added after Bellange's name.

63 Reproduced in Sylvestre 1981, p. 221.

64 Thuillier in Nancy 1992. See also J. Thuillier, 'La vie et l'oeuvre de J. De Bellange', *Annuaire du Collège de France* 1991/2, pp. 821–36; Reed in the exhibition catalogue, *The French Renaissance in Prints from the Bibliothèque Nationale de France*, Grunwald Center for the Graphic Arts, Los Angeles 1994, p. 446.

65 This argument is developed further in the relevant catalogue entries: see no. 14 and the introduction to nos 17–28.

66 An inventory of the primatial church dated 31 March 1645 identifies the painting on the high altar as 'a large image of the Annunciation given by Duke Henri from the hand of the famous painter Michelangelo'. A provisional primatial church was opened for worship in 1609 and dedicated to the Annunciation (F.-G. Pariset, *Georges de la Tour*, Paris 1948, pp. 108–10, n. 13, p. 364). Caravaggio's painting, now in the Musée des Beaux-Arts, Nancy, is usually dated between 1608 and 1610. A summary of opinion about the painting and how it might have come to Nancy is given by Stefania Macioce ('Caravaggio a Malta e I suoi referenti: notizie d'archivio', *Storia dell'Arte*, 81 1994, p. 220, n. 22). The most likely explanation is that it was a private commission made on behalf of Henri by one of his relations who was in touch with Caravaggio, such as his brother-in-law Cardinal Ferdinando Gonzaga, or his illegitimate son the Count of Brie who would have had the opportunity on Malta in 1608 when he and Caravaggio were fellow candidates for the order of the Knights of Saint John.

67 Choné 1991, p. 179.

68 The sonnet by Jean de Rosières is quoted in full in Worthen–Reed 1975, p. 14. Briefly, it relates how Bellange, in his desire to make a masterpiece for posterity, wanted to paint the portrait of Venus and therefore needed to see her; Venus told him to look at Marguerite because 'elle est Venus en Terre, et je la suis aux Cieux'.

69 See the comments under cat. nos 32–5.

70 Choné even goes so far as to compare the habit of cross-dressing in the ballets – including men dressed as Venus – with the androgynous looking figures in Bellange's prints, Choné 1991, p. 183.

71 See Choné 1991, p. 183. In 1594 all the accessories for the ballet were made for the first time in the Ville-Neuve.

72 See Choné 1991, pp. 61, 66–7 and 72, where Veronica's headdress, or 'bern', which also appears later in the works of Lallemand, Callot and La Tour, is identified as that worn by gypsies.

73 A portrait of Marguerite in oriental dress is identified by Choné as possibly the portrait by Bellange praised in the 1606 sonnet; see Choné 1991, p. 420, n. 95.

74 For instance, Philippe Lonicer, *Chronicorum turcicorum…*, Frankfurt 1578, with illustrations by Jost Amman.

75 At least two of Bellange's prints were made for Nicolas Barnet who was responsible for the restoration of one of the religious orders in Lorraine; see cat. nos 3 and 7.

76 René Tavenaux, 'La Lorraine, terre de catholicité', in Nancy 1992, p. 46.

77 Choné 1991, p. 212.

78 Choné 1991, pp. 247–8. This pilgrimage was established by Archduke Albert and Isabella, who built a church there and presented to Charles the wooden statue, which is mentioned in an inventory of his collection in 1607.

79 Choné 1991, p. 80. The motto of the Dukes of Lorraine, *Fecit potentiam*, which also featured on René's standard, comes from the Virgin's Magnificat: 'He hath shown strength with his arm; He hath scattered the proud in the imagination of their hearts.' (Luke 1:51.)

80 The church was completed in 1629; Nicolas Julet's *Miracles et grâces de Notre-Dame-de-Bon-Secours-lès-Nancy*, with a frontispiece by Callot, appeared in 1630. See Louis Châtellier, 'La Vie Religieuse à Nancy', in *Actes du colloque Jacques Callot 25–7 Juin 1992*, Paris 1993, pp. 170–71, 173.

81 Choné 1991, p. 178.

82 Tavenaux in Nancy 1992, p. 46.

83 Châtellier, op. cit., p. 169. Again the Jesuits tried to control this veneration and taught, for example, that Saint Nicolas was not only a protector of infants but also an example of perfect orthodoxy; see Tavenaux, loc. cit.

84 See Tavenaux in Nancy 1992, pp. 48, 52, and Choné 1991, pp. 305, 521, 756–8. A hermit living in one of the several hermitages outside the walls of Nancy from 1605 to 1636

specialised in translating the great works of the Spanish mystics. In the case of El Greco, with whom Bellange has often been compared, distortions of proportion and the use of light have convincingly been shown as quite precise reflections of Neoplatonic texts that describe the optical appearance of heavenly forms, the flame-like shape of celestial figures, and the mystical effect of light (see J. G. Lemoine, 'La Luz en los cuadros del Greco', *Revista de las ideas estéticas*, 45, 1954; and David Davies, *El Greco*, Oxford 1976). These ideas even spilled over into art theory: in his influential treatise *Trattato dell'arte della pittura* (1584) Giovanni Paolo Lomazzo recommended that ideal figures should not only be elongated but should resemble 'the flame of fire…for it has a "conus" or sharp point with which it seems to divide the air so that it may ascend to its proper sphere' (quoted in Davies).

85 See Choné 1991, pp. 441, 513–21, especially the description of the Jesuit festivities with fireworks in 1623, and the sermons on the Incarnation by André de l'Auge given in 1619.

86 The Yale drawing is reproduced in Worthen–Reed, 1975, p. 42; the Stockholm drawing is reproduced in Nancy 1992, no. 110a.

87 In the case of cat. no. 10, his largest plate, he did not have a piece of paper large enough and had to print the proof on two sheets joined. All the single figures are of almost identical format, probably relating to the convenient size to fit a half-sheet of paper. Some of them may have been etched on either side of the same plate for reasons of convenience and economy.

88 Choné 1991, p. 411.

89 Choné 1991, p. 411.

90 Francesca Consagra, *The De Rossi Print Publishing Shop: a study in the history of the print industry in XVIth century Rome*, PhD. John Hopkins University 1993, pp. 282–6.

91 See Wüthrich, loc. cit. (in note 52), nos 85–95. Wüthrich provides very good reasons for dating the copies to around 1615.

92 Sold at Christie's, London, 29 June 1977, lot 23, and later in Frederick Mulder catalogue 4, *Old Master and Modern Prints*, 1977 no. 2.

93 Cassiano's collection is described in Antony Griffiths, 'The print collection of Cassiano dal Pozzo', *Print Quarterly*, VI 1989, pp. 2–10. This etching is in the volume in the Royal Library at Windsor Castle called 'Dutch Drolls'.

94 Consagra, op. cit., p. 566.

95 See M. Grivel, *Le Commerce de l'estampe à Paris au XVIIe siècle*, Geneva 1986, pp. 401–3. Much of Le Blond's production was anonymous and is described under his name as publisher in the *Inventaire* of the Bibliothèque Nationale.

96 See Maxime Préaud and others, *Dictionnaire des éditeurs d'estampes à Paris sous l'Ancien Régime*, Paris 1987, p. 203.

97 See I. M. Veldman, 'Keulen als toevluchtsoord voor Nederlandse kunstenaars', *Oud Holland* 107 1993, pp. 34–58, esp. pp. 48 and 51.

98 It is worth noting that in 1599 de Passe issued a portrait engraving of Antonia, Duchess of Cleves (Franken 540); the lettering states that he made the drawing of her 'from the life'.

Antonia (1568–1610) was a daughter of Charles III of Lorraine, and this establishes a link between de Passe and Lorraine.

99 Information from Paulette Choné.

100 Other elements are visible in this curious print. The profile woman with an elaborate hairstyle behind the Virgin seems to come directly from one of Chuppin's masquers, while the woman with a basket on her head in the background looks forward to the four etchings of *Hortulanae*.

101 According to the researches of M. Sylvestre, prints by the Sadelers were often copied by painters of the second rank in Lorraine (quoted by Choné 1991, p. 413).

102 See A.-P.-F. Robert-Dumesnil, *Le Peintre-Graveur Français*, Paris 1835–71, VIII p. 144, nos 5 and 6.

103 P. Nérot, 'Une gravure inédite de Jean Appier dit Hanzelet', *Le Pays Lorrain*, 1971 pp. 45–7; J. Choux, 'Jean Appier et Barthélemy Spranger', *Le Pays Lorrain*, 1982, pp. 115–18. The Muller engraving is of Minerva and Mercury arming Perseus for his encounter with Medusa.

104 The best study of Barocci's work is the essay by Louise S. Richards in *The Graphic Art of Federico Barocci: Selected Drawings and Prints*, the catalogue of an exhibition held at the Cleveland Museum of Art and Yale University Art Gallery in 1978.

105 On Salimbeni see Sue Welsh Reed and Richard Wallace, *Italian Etchers of the Renaissance and Baroque*, Museum of Fine Arts, Boston 1989, pp. 98–102.

106 P. J. Mariette, *Abécédario*, ed. P. de Chennevières and A. de Montaiglon, Paris 1853, vol. I p. 110 (= *Archives de l'Art Français*, II).

107 Quoted from Walch 1971, p. 20. This and the following paragraphs are indebted to her second chapter, 'Bellanges Bewertung in der Literatur', pp. 19–29.

108 See L. Betcherman, 'The York House collection and its keeper', *Apollo*, 92 1970, pp. 250–59.

109 This text is most conveniently republished by Marianne Grivel in her monograph *Le Commerce de l'Estampe à Paris au XVIIe siècle*, Geneva 1986, pp. 162–5.

110 See Sue Welsh Reed, 'Après Bellange et Callot; la diffusion du maniérisme lorrain chez les graveurs français du XVIIe siècle', *Actes du colloque Jacques Callot 25–7 Juin 1992*, Paris 1993, pp. 511–32.

111 See Wolfgang Stechow, 'Ludolph Büsinck, a German chiaroscuro master of the seventeenth century', *Print Collector's Quarterly*, XXV 1938, pp. 393–419, and XXVI 1939, pp. 349–59.

112 C. F. Bell (ed.), *Evelyn's Sculptura with the Unpublished Second Part*, Oxford 1906, p. 90.

113 Joachim von Sandrart, *L'Academia Todesca*, Nuremberg 1675, vol. I part 1, p. 80.

114 M. de Marolles, *Catalogue de livres d'estampes et de figures en taille douce*, Paris 1666, p. 60, and Paris 1672, p. 21.

115 Ed. G. Duplessis, Paris 1855. Marolles also mentions Bellange in his *Mémoires*, Paris 1956, p. 157.

116 J. Strutt, *A Biographical Dictionary . . . of Engravers*, London 1785, I p. 80.

117 See note 93. The album of 'Dutch Drolls' also contains a Merian copy of the *Hurdy-Gurdy Player Attacking a Pilgrim* (no. 37). Another album of prints of costume contains Merian's copies of the four *Hortulanae* etchings (fig. 20); this is in the British Library, pressmark 146 i.10; the Merian copies are on f.7.

118 See note 27.

119 P. J. Mariette, *Abécédario*, op. cit. (in note 106), vol. I pp. 109–10, n. 106.

120 Le Père Husson, *Eloge historique de Callot, Noble Lorrain, célèbre graveur, dédié à Son Altesse Royale Monseigneur Charles-Alexandre de Lorraine*, Brussels 1766.

121 F. Basan, *Dictionnaire des Graveurs*, 2nd edn, Paris 1789, p. 59 (1st edn 1767).

122 *Le Peintre-Graveur Français*, V 1841, pp. 81–97. It must be remembered that the 1830s in France had been dominated by battles between the new Romantic school and the classical old guard.

123 F. Courboin, *Histoire Illustré de la Gravure en France*, Paris 1923–9, with four volumes of text and three of plates.

124 Berlin 1922, p. 422.

125 *Kunst und Künstler*, IX 1911, pp. 579ff.

126 *Jahrbuch für Kunstgeschichte des Kunsthistorischen Instituts des Bundesdenkmalamtes*, Band 1 (XV), 1921/2, pp. 22–42. It was later republished in his collected essays, *Kunstgeschichte als Geistesgeschichte* (Art History as History of the Spirit), Munich 1924.

127 Perhaps the most bizarre interpretation of all is in 'Jacques de Bellange ou Le combat avec le diable' by J.-R. Thomé in *Le Courrier Graphique* no. 14, 1938, pp. 21–5. He begins from the proposition that 'tout le drame – le combat avec le démon – se joue dans les profondeurs du subconscient' and goes on from there.

128 O. Benesch, *The Art of the Renaissance in Northern Europe*, Cambridge (Mass.) 1945, pp. 120–21.

129 Anthony Blunt, *Art and Architecture in France 1500–1700*, London 1953. This volume in the Pelican History of Art is still the standard work on the period and is still in print. The passage quoted is on p. 125 of the first edition.

130 John Shearman, *Mannerism*, London 1967, p. 28.

131 In an article in the Viennese journal, *Mitteilungen der Gesellschaft für vervielfältigende Kunst*, 1932, pp. 47–9, Eva Steiner refers to a recent exhibition in the Albertina. Previously, in the same journal in 1930 (p. 15), E. Tietze-Conrat announced that the Albertina collection of 'the great Lorrain artist Jacques Bellange' had just been arranged into an '*erste garnitur*' and a secondary series of '*dubletten*'.

132 The exhibition was shown at the Des Moines Art Center, Iowa, and then at the Museum of Fine Arts, Boston, and the Metropolitan Museum of Art, New York.

133 See *La Bella Maniera: Druckgraphik des Manierismus aus der Sammlung Georg Baselitz*, ed. Ger Luijten, Bern-Berlin 1994.

134 Shown in Los Angeles, New York and Paris in 1994–5.

Catalogue

No precise chronology is attempted. Prints are grouped according to subject, scale and treatment:

Commissions in Nancy: nos 1–3

Religious Prints: nos 3–28

Small-scale prints of the Holy Family (4–9)

Large-scale multi-figure compositions (10–12)

The Death and Resurrection of Christ and the Raising of Lazarus (13–16)

Single Figures: nos 17–36

Christ and the Apostles (17–28)

The Three Magi (29–31)

Secular Subjects: nos 32–40

The *Hortulanae* (32–5)

Hurdy-gurdy players (36–7)

Mythology, Roman history, etc. (38–40)

Except where stated otherwise, all prints are attributed to Jacques Bellange and the exhibits come from the Josefowitz collection. Measurements are taken across the centre of the image and are given in millimetres, height preceding width. In most cases the initial *B* of Bellange's signature can be interpreted as *J* and *B* combined. The numbers cited for watermarks refer to those given for them in that section (pp. 128–35). Quotations from the Bible are taken from the Authorized Version. Principal sources are abbreviated as follows:

Bartsch: Adam Bartsch, *Le Peintre-graveur*, 21 volumes, Vienna 1803–21.

Golden Legend: *The Golden Legend of Jacobus de Voragine*, translated from the Latin by Granger Ryan and Helmut Ripperger, New York 1969.

Hollstein: references to F. W. H. Hollstein, *Dutch and Flemish Echings, Engravings and Woodcuts c.1450–1700*, 1949 continuing; and F. W. H. Hollstein, *German Engravings, Etchings and Woodcuts c.1400–1700*, 1954 continuing.

Lieure: Jules Lieure, *Jacques Callot*, 5 volumes, Paris 1924–7.

Reed: catalogue entries by Sue Welsh Reed in *The French Renaissance in Prints from the Bibliothèque Nationale de France*, exhibition catalogue, Grunwald Center for the Graphic Arts, University of California, Los Angeles 1994.

Thuillier: catalogue entries by Jacques Thuillier in *L'Art en Lorraine au temps de Jacques Callot*, exhibition catalogue, Musée des Beaux-Arts, Nancy 1992.

Walch: Nicole Walch, *Die Radierungen des Jacques Bellange: Chronologie und kritischer Katalog*, Munich 1971.

Worthen–Reed: Amy N. Worthen and Sue Welsh Reed, *The Etchings of Jacques Bellange*, exhibition catalogue, Des Moines Art Center, Des Moines, Iowa 1975.

Wüthrich: L. H. Wüthrich, *Das druckgraphische Werk von Matthäus Merian d. Ä.*, 1, Basel 1966.

1

1 *The Entry of Henri II into Nancy*

Etching. 180 × 486 (sheet trimmed inside platemark).

Walch 1 (only state). Worthen–Reed 1.

This comes from the set of etchings known as the *Pompe funèbre de Charles III* that commemorates not only the funeral of Charles III, which took place in May 1608, but also the entry into Nancy two years later, on 20 April 1610, of Henri II, Charles's successor as Duke of Lorraine. Its publication was of great significance in the history of print-making in Lorraine because it marked the introduction of the art of etching into Nancy (see the Introduction, p. 27). The undertaking was planned by Claude de la Ruelle, who had also been responsible for organising the actual ceremonies, and the etching was carried out by Friedrich Brentel and his young assistant Matthaeus Merian, who were brought to Nancy for the purpose.

This plate, numbered 10 in the sequence of plates headed *L'ordre tenu au marcher, parmy la ville de Nancy capitale de Lorraine, a l'entrée en icelle du sérénissime Prince Henry II*, is a particularly fascinating document, as not only does it give us Bellange's portrait but it also marks his debut as an etcher. As court painter, Bellange took his place among the mounted courtiers accompanying the procession of Henri into Nancy, and he can be seen on the right of this plate, second figure from right in the middle row, looking out at the viewer with round eyes that tell us more about his style than his actual appearance. Walch was the first to notice and propose that the portrait of Bellange on his horse had actually been etched by the artist himself. This wholly convincing attribution is based on the difference of style – the more fluid and spirited line – in comparison with the more staid and organised manner of Brentel and Merian evident in the surrounding figures. The treatment of the face is clearly characteristic of Bellange's style (compare the head of Saint John in no. 5), while the bold handling of the etching needle in the lines and hatching of the horse and drapery is seen in many instances in those

1 (detail)

of his prints where a relatively simple biting – in this case a single bite – is unadorned with stippling or overlaid with complex burnishing and reworking (compare nos 3–5).

The publication of this plate as part of the *Pompe funèbre* means that it must have been etched in the latter part of 1610 or early in 1611, and we can safely assume that this date marked the beginning of Bellange's etched *oeuvre*.

2 *Ex-Libris of Melchior de la Vallée*

Nineteenth-century photogravure from an etching dated 1613.
155 × 101 (plate), 177 × 123 (paper).

Walch 2 (only state). Worthen–Reed fig. 1. Thuillier 33.
British Museum (Franks 8539)

The etching from which this photogravure was made is known in only one impression in the Wiener collection in the Musée Historique Lorrain in Nancy (another impression was destroyed in a fire at the Musée Historique Lorrain in 1871). The photogravure is a good record of the style and general appearance of Bellange's plate, but the process by its nature distorts the fine distinctions and nuance of the etched marks of the original bookplate. The original appears to have been restored in the top right corner, which therefore appears rather odd in the photogravure.

The plate was presumably commissioned in 1613 by Melchior de la Vallée, Cantor and Canon of the Collegiate Church of Saint George in Nancy, and chaplain to Duke Henri II. Melchior's subsequent spectacular fall from grace partly accounts for the rarity of this bookplate. As chaplain, he was a great favourite of Henri and, partly as a result of the duke's attentions, he amassed a fortune, enabling him to lead a life of some opulence: he was therefore in a good position to commission a personal bookplate from Nancy's leading painter. However, the seeds of his downfall were sown when he opposed, unsuccessfully (although rightly as it turned out), the marriage of Henri's daughter Claude to Charles de Vaudémont, son of Henri's brother François. Charles took his devious revenge on Melchior after he succeeded in 1624 as Duke Charles IV. A charge of sorcery was brought against Melchior and he was sentenced to death by burning. This allowed Charles to cast doubt on the validity of his wife's baptism, which had been performed by Melchior, and thereby to dispute the legality of their marriage, which he was seeking to annul! No wonder few people thought fit to preserve Melchior de la Vallée's bookplate.

The architectural design, with a pair of figures on plinths or pedestals, presented rather like statues, framing an inscribed tablet below a coat of arms, was the standard arrangement used throughout Europe for title-pages, and was well established in Lorraine (see Paulette Choné, *Emblèmes et Pensée Symbolique en Lorraine (1525–1633)*, Paris 1991, p.428). It was also adapted for portraits and bookplates (see Aegidius Sadeler's bookplate of Peter Vok,

2

Hollstein 394). It is possible that Bellange had already been involved in designing this sort of work, although the attribution to him of the design of the anonymously engraved title-page of Charles Le Pois' *Makarismos*, published at Pont-à-Mousson by Jacob Garnich in 1609, rests only on stylistic evidence that is far from conclusive (Paulette Choné, *Emblèmes et Pensée Symbolique en Lorraine (1525–1633)*, Paris 1991, fig. 92). In any case that design does not use the architectural frame employed here.

On the left stands the crowned Madonna holding the infant Christ: a slightly less plump infant than usual, but otherwise the group recalls Bellange's several versions of this subject (for instance no. 10). On the other side stands Saint Nicholas, Bishop of Myra (Asia Minor) in the fourth century, whose many miracles multiplied during the growth of his cult in the Middle Ages. At his feet is a tub containing three children – a reference to his best-known miracle in which he restored to life three little boys who had been pickled in brine by a vicious butcher in times of famine. Saint Nicholas was a favourite saint of intercession in Lorraine, and there was a pilgrimage in honour of him to the Lorrainese town of Saint-Nicolas-de-Port (see

3

Paulette Choné, *Emblèmes et Pensée Symbolique en Lorraine (1525–1633)*, Paris 1991, p.149). At the top of the plate a pair of angels holds aloft the coat of arms of Melchior de la Vallée.

This is the only print by Bellange actually dated in the plate. Although most writers have placed it early among his etchings because of its apparently slight and ephemeral nature, Thuillier has pointed out with justification that this sort of small plate, commissioned as a bookplate, can hardly be compared directly with other more ambitious productions without taking their different function and scale into account. Nevertheless, the handling of the etching medium is similar to that seen in Bellange's other plates of this size described under no.3 (figs 22 and 23; Walch 4 and 5, known only in unique impressions in Philadelphia and Boston), while the figures can be compared with the less elaborately etched, smaller-scale, figures in the background of Bellange's larger plates that he may well have etched at around the same time (for instance no. 10).

3 *The Vision of Saint Norbert in Prémontré*

Etching. 210 × 293 (sheet trimmed inside platemark at bottom). Old ink inscription on verso: *Lelandue* [?]. Watermark 12.

Walch 3 (only state). Worthen–Reed 2. Thuillier 7.

Like the bookplate of Melchior de la Vallée (see no. 2), this is an exceptionally rare print. Only two examples have hitherto been recorded: one is in the Bibliothèque Nationale in Paris, and the other, which surfaced around fifteen years ago, is now in the Musée Historique Lorrain in Nancy. This hitherto unpublished third example was discovered only recently in an album of miscellaneous French seventeenth- and eighteenth-century religious prints. Thuillier suggests that the plate remained unfinished, pointing to the blank banderole near the saint and the blank margin at the bottom of the print. However, this impression and the one in Paris show considerable wear in the etched lines and a large number of impressions of the plate must have been printed over many years (the impression in Nancy appears a little stronger). This is supported by the unusual watermark on this impression. The reason that so few examples have survived is that the print was a common votive image and would not have been regarded as an object worth keeping. Blank spaces for inscriptions are found on many of Bellange's plates and so this gives no reason to suppose that the plate was abandoned. As it is unsigned, there are doubtless a few more examples still to be discovered among collections of miscellaneous religious prints.

Saint Norbert (c.1080–1134) was a member of a noble Rhineland family. At the age of about thirty-five he underwent sudden conversion and gave up the life of a princely courtier. He was ordained a priest and travelled as an itinerant preacher. In 1120 he founded a community of 'canons regular' (priests bound by religious vows living in a community under a rule), based on the Augustinian rule, in the valley of Prémontré within the forest of Coucy near Laon. This developed rapidly into the Prémontré (Premonstratensian) Order, or Norbertines. In 1126 Norbert was appointed as Archbishop of Magdeburg. He was formally canonised in 1582.

Norbert's vision occurred one night when he was passing the night in the chapel of Saint John the Baptist in Coucy. The Queen of Heaven appeared and bestowed on him a white habit as a symbol of the Prémontré Order. The order's habit was thus established as a white woollen cloak, or scapular, over a black tunic. They were thence known as White Canons, as opposed to the Black Canons (Augustines). Norbert was more usually shown as Archbishop of Magdeburg, and Callot later made a print of him in this role (Lieure 998). But although the depiction of the vision is rare, it was included as plate 15 of the set of engravings of the life of Saint Norbert published by Theodore Galle (see Hollstein 143–78; the edition in the Fitzwilliam Museum identifies Cornelis Galle as the engraver). Galle's print (fig. 21) shows Norbert in the church in a fairly similar arrangement to Bellange's print, with the Virgin appearing on a cloud holding the Christ Child, who extends his hand in benediction, while two winged angels carry the scapular (in Galle's print the angels are infants). At the top is an inscription from Ecclesiastes 9:8: 'Let thy garments be always white.' In Bellange's print Norbert's vision is set not in the church, which is visible in the background, but in the surrounding forest of Coucy. This allowed him to portray at the same time another legend associated with the local Prémontré Order. A cruel and fierce lion was terrorising people in the forest. An archer asked a hermit to lead him to the beast so that he could slay it, but when he suddenly realised how close they were to the lion he shouted out: 'Tu me l'as de *près montrée*' (you have shown me it [too] close).

In the left foreground is the coat of arms of Nicolas Barnet, Abbot of the Prémontré Abbey of Jovilliers, near Saint-Dizier, from 1592 to 1617. He was an important member of a family associated with the ducal court in Nancy. His father was Jean Barnet, secretary to Charles III until his death in 1591. Undoubtedly Nicolas Barnet commissioned this print as part of the propaganda promoting

Fig. 21 Cornelis Galle (1576–1650), *Saint Norbert*, engraving. 152 × 89 mm. Fitzwilliam Museum, Cambridge

the reform movement among the thirty-eight abbeys of the Prémontré Order in Lorraine in the first two decades of the seventeenth century. Barnet personally sponsored the restoration of Prémontré buildings in western Lorraine that had been almost destroyed by Protestants. His involvement with Bellange's prints evidently went further than this one example, for his arms also appear on the first state of no. 7. As one of the most vigorous of the orders that helped promote elements of the Counter-Reformation in Lorraine, the Norbertines may well have stimulated the production of others among Bellange's devotional plates. The abundant demand for images of popular devotional figures such as the Virgin and various cult saints helps explain the type of religious print that Bellange made.

Worthen points out that the Barnet family was related by marriage to Claude de la Ruelle, who could easily have made the contact between Nicolas Barnet and Bellange after the latter's involvement with the *Pompe Funèbre* (no. 1), in which Nicolas Barnet is depicted. The family had other connections with printmaking. Barnet's brother Louis was in the copper-beating business, and on his death the monopoly for beating copper plates passed to his descendants. The family must have come into close contact with printmakers, publishers and printers; another relation, François Rennel, was later in close contact with Callot (see Paulette Choné, *Emblèmes et Pensée Symbolique en Lorraine (1525–1633)*, Paris 1991, pp. 736 ff.). The Barnet family must have provided Bellange with his etching plates and may well have helped him in other ways when he started etching.

Most writers agree that this print came early in Bellange's etched *oeuvre*. Other rare prints of this sort were probably also associated with local commissions like this and may have been made for Barnet. A unique impression in Philadelphia of a small plate depicting the Virgin herself bestowing the scapular on Norbert (fig. 22, not exhibited), and a unique impression in Boston of Saint Augustine as one of the Church Fathers in prayer (fig. 23, not exhibited) may both have Prémontré connections, for as Worthen points out (Worthen–Reed 4) the figures of Norbert and Augustine (from whose order the Prémontré Order was descended) were often paired on Lorraine title-pages. Like the bookplate of 1613 (see no. 2) and unlike most of Bellange's other plates, none of this group found their way into the hands of Paris publishers, presumably because they became the property of the patron or the commissioning religious foundation.

4 *The Holy Family with Mary Magdalene and Saint Anne*

Etching and engraving. 335 × 241 (sheet trimmed inside platemark). Etched inscription: *Bellange fecit / Inventor*. Watermark 1.

Walch (rejected) pp. 214–53 I/II. Worthen–Reed 23. Thuillier 11. Reed 182.

The attribution of this plate to Bellange has been the subject of some debate, with Walch and Worthen–Reed suggesting that it was completed by someone else, despite the fact that it is signed and that it was among the plates that passed to Le Blond in Paris. More recently, Thuillier

Fig. 22 (above right) Bellange, *The Virgin Bestowing the Scapular on Saint Norbert*, etching (Walch 4). 90 × 75 mm. Philadelphia Museum of Art, the Muriel and Philip Berman gift, acquired from the J. S. Philips bequest of 1876 to the Pennsylvania Academy of Fine Arts

Fig. 23 (below right) Bellange, *Saint Augustine in Prayer*, etching (Walch 5). 108 × 65 mm. Boston, Museum of Fine Arts, Otis Norcross Fund

and Reed have accepted it as entirely Bellange's work, arguing that areas of perceived clumsiness in the drawing can be explained by the artist's unfamiliarity with the etching medium. Thuillier may well be right to suppose that such a relatively straightforward print was made soon after Bellange's introduction to etching in 1610–11 (no. 1), and it seems reasonable to suppose that the technical finesse seen in some of the artist's other prints represents a later development as he refined his means of pursuing elegant silhouettes and serpentine poses. In fact, the uncertain spatial relationship of the figures and the rather flatly modelled drapery seem as characteristic of the artist in certain of his prints as the elaborately distorted hands and the soap-sud curls. The treatment of the hair and faces can be compared to the figures at the top right of no. 3, while another print, *The Holy Family with Saint Catherine, Saint John the Evangelist and an Angel* (no. 5), although technically more complex, shows a similar treatment of composition and modelling of forms: compare the lack of interest in establishing the existence of specific limbs such as Saint Catherine's left leg!

Another factor that influenced the appearance of the print is the nature of its relationship to the preparatory drawing (Yale University Art Gallery, Worthen–Reed 22), one of the few surviving drawings that is clearly connected with a print (see p. 32 above). In this plate and in no. 5 etching is treated essentially as a draughtsman's medium. The etching needle is handled with the boldness and directness with which the artist might make a pen-and-ink drawing (the effect is comparable to pen-and-ink drawings attributable to Bellange, such as that in Frankfurt [reproduced as Thuillier 120], and more particularly to a drawing of the Adoration of the Magi in Munich, reproduced as Thuillier 31a). No. 4 is essentially a simple single-bite etching where only a little retouching has been done with an engraving tool to reinforce the contours of the heads and hands. There is little or none of the softly modelled stippling that is such a feature of many of his other prints. As Reed observes, the single-bite approach, the shallow composition and the insistent construction of areas of hatched line set against patches of blank paper recall certain of the etchings produced by the Fontainebleau school in the mid-sixteenth century (compare the technique of no. 11c).

The subject is also comparable with no. 5, a *sacra conversazione*, with the Holy Family joined by figures traditionally associated and depicted with them but who played no role in the childhood of Christ. In this case the Holy Family, and the Virgin's mother Anne, are joined by the penitent figure of a woman, usually identified as Mary Magdalene, who anoints the infant's feet with her tears and with expensive ointment that she takes from a dish on the ground. This episode took place later in Christ's life when he was either at supper with Simon the Pharisee (Luke 7:36–50) or at the house of Mary and Martha (John 12:3–8). Mary's long hair, which she used to wipe Christ's

feet, identifies her as a reformed courtesan. As she also adopts this pose in depictions of Christ's crucifixion, her inclusion in this print provides the premonition of Christ's sacrifice so often encountered in depictions of his infancy (see also no. 16). She occurs with a comparable gesture in similar types of composition by other artists, for example Correggio's painting of *The Virgin and Child with Saint Jerome and Mary Magdalene* that was reproduced in a number of prints. Mary Magdalene was particularly popular in France due to a story told in the *Golden Legend* that relates how she travelled to Provence and lived there for many years as a hermit (see also no. 14). Her alleged relics, discovered at Vézelay in the thirteenth century, contributed to the growth of her cult, which was particularly strong after the Counter-Reformation.

The device of closing the composition at the top with a curtain was used to some extent in all of Bellange's depictions of the Virgin and Child (nos 4–9), while the idea of Joseph lifting the curtain appears in a number of early seventeenth-century depictions (see Aegidius Sadeler's engraving after Hans von Aachen, Hollstein 79).

5 *The Holy Family with Saint Catherine, Saint John the Evangelist and an Angel*

Etching. 271 × 189 (plate), 274 × 193 (paper). Etched inscription: *Bellange*. Watermark 1.

Walch 15 1/11. Worthen–Reed 20. Thuillier 12.

In terms of subject and composition the print is closely related to no. 4, but the technical means have been refined. The stippling is finer, producing a smoother *sfumato* shading on the flesh, and, instead of contours reinforced with an engraving tool, the darker lines have been produced by etching them for longer in the acid. The fine lines underlying the cross-hatching show that the density of shading was built up in layers with a succession of immersions in the acid (as in many of Bellange's etchings, there are places where the etching ground between the lines has failed and the acid has bitten in pools). Nevertheless, the approach remains similar to no. 4, which suggests on the one hand that this print may be placed relatively early among Bellange's etched work, and on the other that it may well have been based on a similar type of preparatory drawing (Thuillier proposes a painting as a model). The direct influence of the etchings of Parmigianino and his followers is apparent in the depiction of Joseph's face and hair (at top right) which, unusually for Bellange, is constructed almost entirely out of short lines without stippling or cross-hatching.

Saint Catherine of Alexandria is depicted in the foreground with her usual attribute, a section of the spiked wheel on which according to legend her execution was attempted (she was eventually beheaded) in punishment for protesting against the worship of idols and then

5

Fig. 24 Jan Muller (1571–1628) after Bartholomeus Spranger, *The Holy Family Attended by Angels*, engraving *c.*1590. 290 × 213 mm. Fitzwilliam Museum, Cambridge

refusing to marry the emperor Maxentius. Typically Bellange has taken full advantage of the opportunity to depict her with a suitably exotic costume. Her pose and her costume are similar to the *repoussoir* figure at the bottom left corner of Bellange's drawing of a battle now in Munich (reproduced as Thuillier 106). Her rapt gaze fixed on Christ and her lifted hand recall the moment when, in her prison cell, Christ appeared to her in a vision. Catherine became a cult saint in the Middle Ages and was also associated with the cult of the Virgin, with whom she is often represented. Behind Catherine is Saint John the Evangelist, who was also associated with the Virgin: he was the Apostle to whom Jesus on the cross confided the care of his mother. He holds his attribute of a chalice, out of which emerges a dragon (for an explanation of this see the two depictions of the same saint in the series of Apostles, nos 22a and 22b). His pose resembles that of one of the Magi (no. 29a). The angel in the background and the attitude of Joseph (whose hunched pose and crooked features recur with little alteration in no. 10) resemble

types found in Northern Mannerist depictions (see for example Muller's engraving after Spranger, fig. 24; Bartsch 66).

6a *The Virgin and Child with Cradle*

state I

Etching, reinforced by a later hand with pen and ink on the outlines of the cradle. 139 × 211 (sheet trimmed to the edge of image). Formerly laid down on old (eighteenth-century?) backing paper, which has an old inscription about Bellange copied from Strutt's *Dictionary of Engravers* (1785). Watermark 25.

Walch 7 I/III. Worthen–Reed 6. Thuillier 26.
Witt Print Collection, Courtauld Institute Galleries, London.

6b *The Virgin and Child with Cradle*

state II

Etching. 142 × 212 (sheet trimmed inside platemark). Etched inscription: *Bellange* (*ang* reversed).

Walch 7 II/III. Worthen–Reed 6. Thuillier 26.

The unique proof of the unfinished first state (no. 6a) was published and illustrated by Walch, who stated that she knew it only from a photograph in the Witt Library at the Courtauld Institute of Art; subsequent scholars have referred to the illustration in Walch but none has known the location of the print. We are grateful to Richard Godfrey for bringing to our attention that the print itself is in the collection of the Courtauld Institute, where it was formerly filed in the Witt Library. The backing paper shows that it was in England by the eighteenth century.

This proof is of crucial importance for the study of Bellange the printmaker as it is the only known proof before completion of work, with the exception of the unique first state of *Diana and the Hunter* (see no. 38) in the Bibliothèque Nationale. It is less finished than the first state of *The Virgin and Child with a Rose* (which may have been issued in that state; see no. 7) and shows work rather further advanced than is the case in the *Diana and the Hunter* proof. The printing of the Courtauld proof is so faint that on first sight it looks like an impression from a worn plate, but this effect is typical of some of the very first proofs printed from a newly etched plate before the ink has worked its way fully into the lines. A similar effect is seen in the proof (before the artist's lettering) of Barocci's *Annunciation* in the British Museum (illustrated in Antony Griffiths, ed., *Landmarks in Print Collecting*, London 1996, no. 21a). The faint printing makes some of the work on the plate difficult to discern, but most of the light shading, such as the horizontal lines in the sky, has already been etched.

Many areas, such as the shadows on the Virgin's drapery, were overlaid with another layer of hatching in

6a

6b

the second state (no. 6b). The most significant changes were those made to the Virgin's nose and outstretched hand. In the first state her nose had the same concave profile seen on the face of the Virgin in nos 4 and 8a. Perhaps Bellange found it too stark against the child's forehead. In any case, he burnished out the line and reversed the shape of the profile in the second state – traces of the burnishing can be seen on the forehead of the child. At the same time he lowered the position of the top of the Virgin's left wrist and forearm while raising the fingers holding the swaddling clothes. This search for a more elegant hand gesture is typical of Bellange and is shown by the traces of alteration to hands and fingers found in several other prints. The extensive burnishing needed to erase the previous work in this area of the plate resulted in the erasure of some of the fluted lines at the bottom of the pilaster in the second state. Other more minor changes include the shading of the wall by the distant figure, which obscures some of the architectural detail sketched in the first state. In addition, the halo is reduced in width on the right: the original line is still just visible in the second state. The rather crude signature was also added in the second state. The soft and subtle shading of the stippled and burnished flesh, and the

carefully judged pattern of hatching and highlights on the drapery, are entirely characteristic of Bellange's mature etching style, which varies little in the following prints (nos 7–9).

The depiction of the Virgin with a cradle and a distant figure, often seen through a doorway and identifiable as Joseph, occurs in numerous late sixteenth- and seventeenth-century prints of the Holy Family in Egypt (for example, Jan Sadeler after F. Sustris, Hollstein 303). Walch (p. 80, quoted also in Worthen–Reed) notes that elements of the composition seem to derive from a print of the *Madonna and Child* (Bartsch 6) by Ventura Salimbeni, which is now considered a copy of an etching by Guido Reni. Bellange could have known either print by 1613 (the date of the deaths of both Salimbeni and the Roman publisher of Reni's etching, Nicolo van Aelst). But although either of these could have provided a precedent for the arrangement of the architectural setting, with an opening at the back where the figure of Joseph is seen, the group of the Virgin and Child is quite different. The pose of the Child is virtually a repetition of that found in another print by Bellange showing the Virgin wrapping the Child in swaddling clothes (fig. 25, not exhibited), which lacks the technical refinement of this print and is probably earlier.

The infant Christ is shown holding an apple, the fruit of the Tree of Knowledge, which was a common allusion in such depictions to Christ's role as the future redeemer of mankind from original sin. The cat was another frequent inclusion in prints of the Virgin and Child (see for example no. 8c), although whether it always carries an intentional symbolism of the devil, or an association with night or sleep, is difficult to establish. The elaborately carved cradle at first looks like either another piece of obscure symbolism or typical Bellange whimsy, but it is neither: cradles of an almost identical design appear in many early seventeenth-century prints (see, for example, Jan Saenredam's engraving *Night* after Goltzius, Bartsch 94, which also includes a cat). Although the identification of the distant figure as Joseph is reasonably inferred from other prints of this subject, he is here rather enigmatic, to say the least, resembling the mysterious figures wandering anonymously about in the background of Bellange's larger prints (see no. 16).

Fig. 25 Bellange, *The Virgin Wrapping the Child in Swaddling Clothes*, etching (Walch 8). 185 × 104 mm. Boston, Museum of Fine Arts, Otis Norcross Fund

7 *The Virgin and Child with a Rose*

Etching. 212 × 142 (sheet trimmed inside platemark, Le Blond's address at bottom cut off). Etched inscription: *.Bellange. fecit.* (*n* reversed or joined to *g*).

Walch 25 II/II [III/III]. Worthen–Reed 43. Thuillier 30.

This was etched on a plate the same size as that used for no. 6. At the bottom of the image is the trace of the coat of arms of Nicolas Barnet (see no. 3), which can be seen before erasure on the unique impression of the first state in

·kellarge·fecit·

7

Boston; this was unknown to Walch and first described by Sue Welsh Reed (*Print Quarterly*, IX 4, 1992, pp. 383–6, fig. 202). The reappearance of the same coat of arms as that etched on no. 3 suggests that this plate may also have been etched for Barnet as a commission connected with the reforming Prémontré Order in Lorraine. The impression of the first state has most of the lower margin trimmed, but it is evident that it lacks the signature. In the second state (Walch's first state) Bellange added the signature, erased the coat of arms and adjusted the shading. He added diagonal lines over some of the highlights of the drapery such as the Virgin's right knee, extra cross-hatching in most of the background, and clarifying touches to the faces, the Virgin's hair and the Virgin's hand holding the rose. The alterations to the Virgin's other hand, which are comparable to those in nos 6a and 6b, had already been made in the first state. In the third state (Walch's second) the only addition is Le Blond's address.

It is evident from these alterations that Bellange himself was responsible for the removal of the coat of arms, and we can only speculate on the circumstances that occasioned this. Two hypotheses present themselves: firstly, that a fair number of impressions of the first state were printed for Barnet but that, unlike no. 3 (which was more specifically related by subject to the Prémontré Order), the plate remained in Bellange's possession and he altered it in line with his developing style in nos 6–9 before printing a second edition; alternatively, that the plate was at first intended for Barnet but that for some reason Bellange changed his mind while still in the process of finishing the plate and therefore removed Barnet's arms before the plate was issued. The scribbled lines in the margin at bottom left apparently show Bellange testing the etching ground with his needle before working on the plate or perhaps before adding the signature. Although there are no signs of erased coats of arms on Bellange's other religious prints, one or more of them may have also started life as a private commission for Barnet or another patron or religious foundation.

The Virgin was often depicted with a rose in prints after both Northern and Italian designs (see, for example, Aegidius Sadeler's engravings after Parmigianino [Hollstein 74] and Marten de Vos [Hollstein (de Vos) 741] or Raphael Sadeler's engraving after Annibale Carracci [Hollstein 58]), although it is sometimes the infant Christ who actually holds the flower (see for example Jan Sadeler's print for the Society of Jesus [Hollstein 283] or Jan Muller's engraving after Spranger [Bartsch 66]). An early Christian legend mentioned by Saint Ambrose tells how the rose grew without thorns until the Fall of Man and his expulsion from Paradise. It therefore became associated with the Virgin who was called 'the rose without thorns' because of her sinless state and her own Immaculate Conception, which fitted her to be Mother of Christ. In the sixteenth century she was often linked with a

passage from the Song of Songs, which sometimes appears as an inscription on prints of this type (see Jan Sadeler's print, Hollstein 286): 'I am the rose of Sharon, And the lily of the valleys. As the lily among thorns, so is my love among the daughters.'

8a *The Virgin and Child with Distaff and an Angel*

Etching and engraving. 255 × 186 (sheet trimmed inside platemark). Etched inscription: *.Bellange. fecit.* (n joined to g). Watermark 1.

Walch 9 II/III. Worthen–Reed 8. Thuillier 41. Reed 143.

An earlier state exists before the addition of the signature. It is known in only two impressions (Albertina, Vienna, and Prouté collection, Paris) which are both printed with a lot of tone, and the Paris impression has very inky edges suggesting that it is a proof prior to the signed published edition. Undoubtedly there would have been still earlier working states that have not survived. There must surely, for example, have been proofs taken before the engraved and etched accents were added *over* the etched stippling in areas such as the Virgin's hair and Christ's face.

Reed draws attention to the possible influence of Barocci's print of *The Annunciation* (no. 8b) on the setting in this print. The closest points of similarity are the window at the back, which Bellange seems to have closed off at the left during work on the print, and the divine light coming through the drapes above. But it is the technical example of Barocci's prints that would have given Bellange most reason to study them, particularly the carefully built-up layers of hatching combined with stippling, and the use of an engraving tool to provide final accents and adjustments. A similar combination of hatching and stippling appears in the etchings of Salimbeni (no. 8c). (For further discussion of the technical relationship between Barocci, Salimbeni and Bellange see the Introduction, p. 39.) Thuillier ignores the close connection with prints by other artists and supposes that no. 8a was based on a cabinet painting. But the work is so perfectly conceived in terms of etching that it seems unnecessary to suppose that the print was dependent on a painted model. The variety of etched marks and their subtle modulation by burnishing on the lit area of the Virgin's drapery is particularly remarkable. Most magical is the depiction of the fragile thread represented by a single etched line that meanders unbroken across patches of shading and blank paper.

The subject of the Virgin spinning thread while the Christ Child sleeps was quite common in scenes of the Holy Family in Egypt, and Reed points to Dürer's woodcut (Bartsch 90) as one such example; another is the print by Jan Sadeler cited in no. 6 (Hollstein 303). The distaff and basket of wool (shown in the lower right of this print and also visible in no. 9) had become associated with the

8a

8b

8c

Virgin through a legend telling of her upbringing in the Temple of Jerusalem, where she would spin and weave the priests' vestments.

FEDERICO BAROCCI (1526–1612)

8b *The Annunciation*

Etching and engraving, after his own painting of 1582–4. 438 × 310 (sheet trimmed within platemark). Watermark: lily in a circle (cf. Briquet 7127).

Bartsch XVII 2.1.

VENTURA SALIMBENI (*c.*1568–1613)

8c *Saint Agnes*

Etching. 212 × 158 (sheet trimmed to platemark).

Bartsch XVII 194.7.
British Museum (v. 3–19, bequeathed by
Rev. C. M. Cracherode).

9 *The Annunciation*

Etching and engraving. 339 × 320 (sheet trimmed just inside platemark). Engraved inscription: *Bellange Eques incidit.* Watermark 22b.

Walch 24 II/III. Worthen–Reed 42. Thuillier 42. Reed 194.

The subject comes from Luke's Gospel: 'And the angel came in unto her, and said, Hail, thou that art highly favoured, the Lord is with thee: blessed art thou among women.... Fear not Mary: for thou hast found favour with God. And, behold, thou shalt conceive in thy womb, and bring forth a son, and shalt call his name Jesus.' (1:28–31.) Mary's questioning gesture suggests the continuation of this passage: 'Then said Mary unto the angel, How shall this be, seeing I know not a man? And the angel answered and said unto her, The Holy Ghost shall come upon thee...therefore also that holy thing which shall be born of thee shall be called the Son of God.' (34–5.) The lily held by the angel is the traditional attribute of the archangel Gabriel, and also a symbol of the Virgin's purity. Gabriel is often shown arriving while the Virgin is reading (note the open book on the stool). The subject had a special resonance in Nancy (see above p. 31 and note 79).

Bellange Eques inuenit.

9

The Virgin's face and demeanour recall numerous prints of the same subject (for example no. 8b, or the etching by Salimbeni, Bartsch 4). The angel, however, seems to have been directly inspired by Caravaggio's painting of *The Annunciation* (Musée des Beaux Arts, Nancy), which had been given by Henri II to the newly founded primatial church (see note 66, p. 46 above). The dark tenebrist style of Caravaggio's painting, datable to 1608–10, must have caused a sensation when the work arrived in Nancy, or at least when it was put up in the church – perhaps when the provisional building was opened for worship in 1609 or soon afterwards. In any case, as court painter, Bellange must have seen it as soon as it arrived. The similarities between the angels in the two works are striking: the elevated position resting on a cloud, the position of the wings, the long outstretched arm reaching downwards, the raised forefinger, the position of the lily, and the sash knotted behind the back. Bellange even evokes something of the dramatic spotlighting of the angel's shoulder and rear, although the forms are more artificially elegant and the length of the angel's arm exaggerated, compared with the relative naturalism of Caravaggio's painting.

As observed in no. 8a, engraved flicks have been added over the etched stippling in the Virgin's face, and these are lacking in the unique impression in Boston of the first state before inscription. There is even more variety in the type and combination of mark than in no. 8a, giving a greater differentiation of textures. The preliminary outline of the angel's wings is visible at the top, suggesting that they were at first intended to be positioned slightly differently.

The impression of the first state in Boston is printed on paper with a crowned H watermark which was only introduced in April 1613 (see p. 130), so it can be reliably inferred that the print was made after this date. The same paper was used for the earliest impressions of nos 12 and 14. No. 14 also shares the same form of inscription in the second state.

10 *The Adoration of the Magi*

Etching and engraving. 596 × 429 (sheet trimmed inside platemark). Etched inscription: *Bellange. fecit.* (*g* reversed). Watermark 9.

Walch 20 II/v. Worthen–Reed 31–2. Thuillier 31b. Reed 190.

This is Bellange's largest print. He obviously did not keep paper this large in stock, as the unique proof of the first state before signature (now in Ottawa) is printed on two sheets of paper joined across the centre. Considerable alterations had already been made to the plate before any of the surviving states were printed, most notably the erasure of a distant towered city (similar to that in no. 39) crowned with a star: remnants of the previous work are still visible in the blank sky in this state. Later in the seventeenth century the plate passed into the hands of the

Parisian publisher van Merle who issued it with his address of 1651–82, adding distant hills and a star in the blank sky, and a Latin inscription in the lower margin based on Matthew 2:11: 'And when they were come into the house, they saw the young child with Mary his mother, and fell down, and worshipped him: and when they had opened their treasures, they presented unto him gifts; gold, and frankincense, and myrrh.' In the final fifth state, probably dating from the very end of the century, the plate was radically altered, particularly the Virgin's head, which was made less tall: evidently Bellange's weird proportions had to be tamed to accord with changes of taste.

The scene of the Three Wise Men bearing gifts from the east was one of the few subjects officially sanctioned by the Counter-Reformation that gave artists license to portray opulence and luxurious display. Since the fifteenth century it was also established as a subject that gave artists the opportunity to experiment with compositions involving figures viewed from behind and horses going in and out of the picture space. Typically Bellange seized this opportunity with relish, sparing no extravagance in either the depiction of exotic costumes, headdresses and precious vessels, or in the amazing amalgam of poses and gestures. In the foreground is a line-up of rear views: one of the Magi, a servant boy with a parrot on his shoulder, and a horseman shown in bold foreshortening, his hand projecting towards us out of the picture plane. These conceits – the audacious rear views and the daring foreshortening – were elements that Bellange employed almost with abandon by the time he turned to etching, probably adopting them from the Mannerist prints of Goltzius and his school. In his earlier composition of *The Adoration of the Magi*, engraved by Crispin de Passe around 1600 (fig. 12), many elements appear that are typical of late sixteenth-century compositions, and some of these, such as the step in the foreground and the group of the first wise man bowing in homage to the Virgin and Child, are similar to the equivalent passages in this print. Here, however, as in his other two largest prints (nos 11a and 12), the main protagonists are placed at the very centre of the composition (the exact centre is actually the Virgin's knee), and around them is a convoluted vortex of figures – disparate groups held together by sheer energy of invention. Also lacking in the earlier print are the outrageous backsides in the foreground, although these too are a late sixteenth-century convention taken to extremes. Another version of the subject by Bellange, a pen-and-ink drawing now in Munich (Thuillier 31a), has been cited as a possible preparatory drawing for the composition preserved in the print, but it has few similarities and the design recalls rather the enclosed type of composition seen in nos 4 and 5.

Bellange took up the theme again in his set of prints of the Three Magi (nos 29a–31a), while the figure seen from the rear at the lower right of the print was copied by Merian in his set of the Three Magi after Bellange (no. 30b). The boy with the parrot (which recalls a similar

Bellange fecit

10

figure in an Adoration engraved by Agostino Carracci after Baldassare Peruzzi; Bartsch 11) and other elements of Bellange's print were included, with variations, in a design by Crispin de Passe engraved by his son Willem (Hollstein 4) after Bellange's death.

Another notable feature of the print is the fragmentary sculpture in the top right background, balancing the classical column on the left, because it seems to be Bellange's own invention. Although it is broken as if in imitation of an antique sculpture, it does not seem to reflect a direct ancient source. The closest ancient precedents are the groups known as *Pasquino* (thought at the time either to represent Hercules overcoming Geryon or Alexander the Great holding up the wounded soldier Pasquino), and in particular the most fragmentary version in Rome that was frequently illustrated from the sixteenth century onwards (see Francis Haskell and Nicholas Penny, *Taste and the Antique*, Yale 1981, no. 72, fig. 153). Far more striking, however, is the kinship of the Bellange group with the various allegorical marble groups depicting one figure triumphing over another carved in Florence in the middle of the sixteenth century, such as Vincenzo Dante's *Honour and Falsehood* or Pierino da Vinci's *Samson Slaying a Philistine*, which derived their formal and allegorical ideas from Michelangelo (J. Pope-Hennessy, *Italian High Renaissance and Baroque Sculpture*, London 1963, plates 77 and 62). There is no evidence that Bellange ever saw these sculptures, but he probably knew the idea through prints or bronze statuettes (see Pope-Hennessy, p. 78 and fig. 128). The format spread to northern Europe and Adrian de Vries was still adapting it for a bronze statuette in 1612 (Lars O. Larsson, *Adrian de Vries*, Vienna 1967, plate 147). Bellange's group differs in that the upper figure is not upright but itself seems to be oppressed from above (indeed it seems oppressed by the proximity of the top edge of the plate!). Nevertheless, he probably intended a Victory allegory, to represent an analogy of the triumph of the new order over the old, a common theme of Nativity or Adoration scenes.

11a *Christ Carrying the Cross*

Etching and engraving. 407 × 581 (sheet trimmed inside plate mark). Engraved inscription: *Bellange Eques in incide* (within the image), *Vere languores nostros ipse tulit, et dolores nostros, ipse portauit et nos putauimus eum quasi leprosum et percussum a Deo et humiliatum: Ipse autem vulnerat<us>est propter iniquitates nostras, attrotus [attritus] est propter scelera <nostra>: disciplina pacis nostrae super eum, et livore eius sancti [sanati] sumus* (in lower margin). Watermark 24.

Walch 23 (only state). Worthen–Reed 40. Thuillier 28. Reed 189.

The Latin inscription in the lower margin is from Isaiah: 'Surely he hath borne our griefs, and carried our sorrows: yet we did esteem him stricken, smitten of God, and afflicted. But he was wounded for our transgressions, he was bruised for our iniquities: the chastisement of our peace was upon him; and with his stripes we are healed.' (Isaiah 53:2.) Thuillier has attempted to play down the influence of Schongauer's masterpiece (no. 11b), rightly emphasised by Reed (in Worthen–Reed) as the inspiration for this print. But none of the alternative examples cited by Thuillier, such as the print by Jean Mignon after Luca Penni (no. 11c), are particularly convincing as models when compared with the many correspondences between the two epic prints by Bellange and Schongauer. It is not only the placement and pose of Christ and the general direction of the procession, but specific correspondences with other figures: the soldier with his back to us holding a spear, the figure laying his hand on the cross, the placement of the prominent figure in front of the cross to the right of Christ, and the rear view of the horse and rider in the middle

Fig. 26 Camillo Procaccini (*c*.1555–1629), *The Transfiguration*, etching *c*.1590. 575 × 345 mm. British Museum

11a

distance to the left of the cross; the two bare-backed thieves at the left of Schongauer's print are placed just beyond the front of the cross in Bellange's version. All of these figures are of course completely reinvented in Bellange's idiom, no doubt with the influence of ideas absorbed from other compositions. One of the figures is transformed in meaning: the man laying his hand on the cross is turned by Bellange from the sneering grotesque seen in Schongauer's print into a sympathetic character identifiable as Simon of Cyrene who was chosen to carry the cross after Jesus (Luke 51:26).

The group of figures that has no basis at all in the Schongauer is that of the various grieving women, one of them protecting her child, at the bottom left corner. These derive from the description in Luke (51:27–9): 'And there followed him a great company of people, and of women, which also bewailed and lamented him. But Jesus turning unto them said, Daughters of Jerusalem, weep not for me, but weep for yourselves, and for your children.' One of these women leans forward proffering a handkerchief: this is Veronica, the woman of Jerusalem who was filled with compassion at the sight of Christ suffering on the way to Calvary, and wiped his face with a veil, on which was left

a miraculous image of Christ's face. The story had no biblical basis but was commonplace in depictions of this subject (see for instance the Mignon, no. IIc). The town depicted in the right distance is intended as Jerusalem although it is compiled with a sprinkling of features more closely resembling Rome – particularly the Trajanic column.

As in his other two grand multi-figure prints (nos 10 and 12), the main protagonist is made the very centre of the picture, a point of rest amid the swirl of the composition, and a powerful point of formal and spiritual focus. Christ's head appears faint in all impressions, although in many cases (but not this impression) collectors over the centuries have attempted to strengthen the lines with pen and ink, assuming (as does Thuillier) that the faintness is due to a defect in the etching. However, as Reed states, Christ's face was not unintentionally underbitten but intentionally burnished so that it printed lighter. The intention was evidently to give Christ a spiritual aura, an other-worldly grace, in much the same way that burnishing was used on Christ's face in Camillo Procaccini's etching of *The Transfiguration* (fig. 26; Bartsch 4) of 1587–90, where it was intended to convey the words: 'and his face did shine as

11b

11c

the sun' (Matthew 17:2). A rather more prosaic piece of burnishing in Bellange's print is on the buttock of the soldier facing away from us where the woman's hand seems to have been altered slightly.

This is one of the instances where Thuillier supposes that the print reproduces a painting by Bellange, but no such painting is known to have existed and the importance of Schongauer's engraving for this composition strengthens the idea that Bellange was in the business of making prints for their own sake. Indeed, the complexity of the etching is closely related to the compositional effects in such passages as the more lightly bitten face that appears beyond the right shoulder of the figure standing with his back to us, or the remarkable blank space, left unetched, between the profile of the other main standing soldier and the hair of the figure beyond. More difficult to explain is the apparently unfinished face on the extreme centre right, which gives some idea of the initial stages of etching before the elaboration of stippling and layers of hatching were added. The ambitious technical devices of Bellange's print make a fascinating comparison with the etching by Jean Mignon (no. 11c), which is a straightforward single-bite etching typical of the prints produced by the etchers associated with the Fontainebleau school.

Martin Schongauer (c.1450–91)

11b *The Road to Calvary*

Engraving. 289 × 435 (sheet trimmed within platemark at bottom).

Lehrs 9.

Jean Mignon (active 1535–c.1555)

11c *The Road to Calvary*

Etching. 368 × 488 (plate), 375 × 496 (paper). Dated in the plate: *1544* (the *5* reversed).

Zerner 29.

12 *The Martyrdom of Saint Lucy*

Etching and engraving. 457 × 349 (plate, trimmed slightly on right), 464 × 351 (paper). Etched inscription: *Bellange*. Watermark 18.

Walch 16. Worthen–Reed 29. Thuillier 29.

The historical figure of Lucy (Lucia) was a fourth-century martyr at Syracuse in Sicily, probably in Diocletian's persecution. She was venerated at an early date, and by the end of the Middle Ages colourful threads of legend had been woven around her life. The *Golden Legend* tells how

she enraged her fiancé by distributing her wealth to the poor in gratitude for the miraculous healing of her mother at the shrine of Saint Agatha. He denounced her as a Christian to the magistrate Paschasius and, when she refused to recant, she was tied to a team of oxen to be dragged to a brothel, but miraculously they were unable to move her. After amazingly surviving many other tortures – burning alive, molten lead poured in her ears, and boiling oil, pitch and urine – she was finally killed by a friend of Paschasius, who plunged a dagger or sword through her throat.

Bellange shows Lucy with her hands tied (perhaps a remnant of being tied to the team of oxen) and with a dagger through her throat. According to the *Golden Legend,* she did not die immediately but announced that Diocletian was overthrown and peace was restored to the Church. Various figures point into the distance, perhaps signalling the arrival of the envoys from Rome, who, according to the *Golden Legend,* came to arrest Paschasius. There is little other trace of narrative detail, and it is difficult to identify specific figures other than the martyr. Those eighteenth-century writers who mention another plate of similar size representing the martyrdom of Virginia, the Roman virgin martyr who was also stabbed to death rather than lose her chastity, were no doubt simply recording a misinterpretation of this plate. The stories are similar, but the fact that Bellange shows the martyr with a nimbus signals that she is a saint and therefore rules out Virginia. Although other martyred virgin saints (Agnes for instance) were similarly depicted, one of Lucy's chief symbols – the burning oil-lamp – is held prominently by the statue of Diana raised at top left. Diana was Roman goddess of chastity and therefore symbolises one of Lucy's virtues as well as representing the pagan idols that she refused to worship. The oil-lamp alludes to Lucy's name. To quote the *Golden Legend*:

Lucy means light. Light has beauty in its appearance; for by its nature all grace is in it, as Ambrose writes. It has also an unblemished effulgence; for it pours its beams on unclean places and yet remains clean.... By this we are to understand that the virgin Lucy was endowed with a stainless purity of life; that in her was an effusion of heavenly love without any unclean desire; that she followed a straight way in her devotion to God, and a long way in daily good works without weakening and without complaint. Or again, Lucy means *lucis via*, the way of light.

Various attempts have been made to suggest other pictures that Bellange may have ransacked for this composition, but none of them are at all convincing, except Walch's comparison with Anton Eisenhoit's *Ecce Homo* engraved in 1590 after Taddeo Zuccaro, and only because it shows the same typical Mannerist device of framing the bottom of the pictures with half-length figures. The actual figure-types are much closer to those in prints by the Northern Mannerists: for instance, the soldier at bottom right can be compared with the foreground figure in Jan

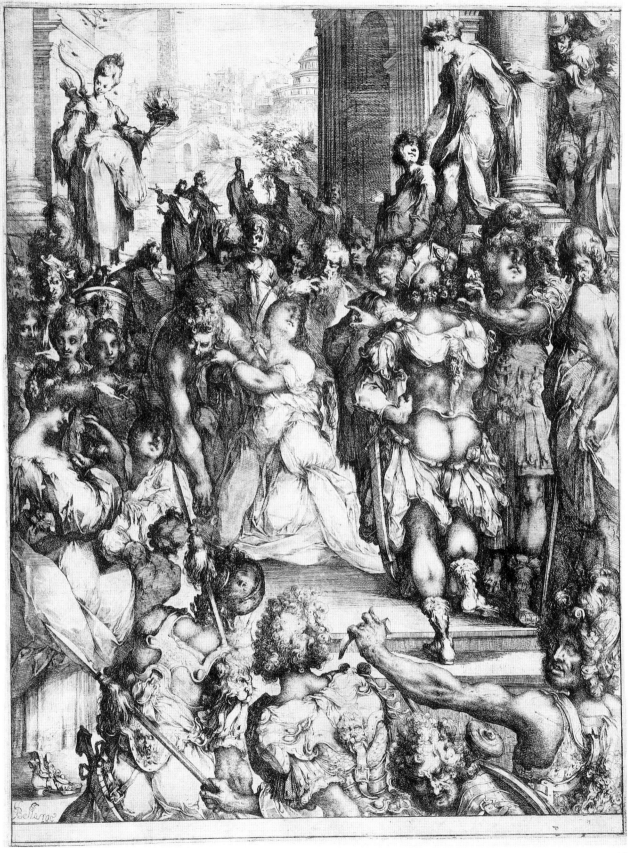

Fig. 27 Jan Muller (1571–1628) after Bartholomeus Spranger, *Minerva and Hermes Arming Perseus*, engraving 1604. 568 × 398 mm. British Museum

Muller's engraving of *Balthasar and the Sacred Vessels* (Bartsch 1), and the figure of Perseus in Muller's engraving after Spranger (fig. 27; Bartsch 69) also provides various consonances of pose. Many of the figures and groupings echo those found in Bellange's other larger prints, particularly nos 10 and 11a, which also have figures at the bottom leading into the picture. Lucy is placed near the centre of the composition in a similar way to the Virgin and Child in no. 10, while her pose resembles that of the reclining figure in no. 39 and the woman at the left of no. 11a. The figure on the step with his back to us also appears with variations in nos 11a and 39. The woman's foot just above the signature is shod with one of the extraordinary antique bootees worn by the *Hortulana* figures (see especially nos 34 and 35), although in other respects she resembles the central figure in no. 13.

A very early impression of the print (Prouté collection, Paris), with the smudgy margins that often imply a proof impression, seems to lack some of the burnishing found in later impressions. This is particularly evident in the hand holding Lucy's hair, which has apparently been burnished to make it more distinct, but some of the highlights on the faces in the middle ground may also have been burnished. The Prouté impression is printed on paper with a crowned H watermark which was only introduced in April 1613 (see p. 130), so it can be reliably inferred that the print was made after this date; the same paper was used for rare first-state impressions of nos 9 and 14. Unlike Bellange's other large plates (nos 10, 11a and 16), this plate is signed with the florid autograph signature found on the *Hortulanae* prints and the set of the Three Magi (nos 29–35).

13 *Three Holy Women*

Etching and engraving. 322 × 207 (sheet trimmed inside platemark at top). Etched inscription: *Bellangelus. Eques / In. fe.*

Walch 22 (only state). Worthen–Reed 38. Thuillier 39.

This print was one of only two devotional prints by Bellange that were copied by Merian (fig. 10; see also no. 15). The copy is inscribed with a quotation from Mark 16 identifying the subject as the Three Holy Women visiting Christ's tomb: 'And when the Sabbath was past, Mary Magdalene, and Mary the mother of James, and Salome, had bought sweet spices, that they might come and anoint him.' In keeping with this subject, Merian changes the figure on the right of Bellange's print so that she is carrying an ointment jar instead of a martyr's palm, and gives her a halo. In Bellange's print the exact identity of the women is not at all clear: all that the iconography tells us is that there are two saints and a martyr. Comparison with the artist's two known treatments of the visit to the tomb (see no. 14) does not really help. Perhaps an inscription in the lower margin would have elucidated the subject, but this part of the print remained blank. Thuillier may well be right when he proposes that the women are Christian equivalents of the three Graces of antiquity, ideals of spiritual beauty clothed in courtly refinement, linked in a ring by the gestures of their arms and hands. But the distinction between martyr and canonised saints suggests that Bellange perhaps may have had something more specific in mind.

Pariset compares the print to *The Three Holy Women Visiting the Tomb* engraved in 1600 by Aegidius Sadeler after Bartholomeus Spranger (fig. 17; Hollstein 60), and there are indeed vivid echoes of poses and the rhythmic relationship between the figures (F.-G. Pariset, 'Bellange et Lagneau ou le maniérisme et le réalisme en France après 1600', *Studies in Western Art*, vol. III, Princeton 1966, p. 125). There are also similarities of poses with the engraving after Goltzius of *Mercury Enamoured of Herse*, from the series illustrating Ovid's *Metamorphoses* (Bartsch 67). But as usual the closest points of contact are with Bellange's own work: the central figure recalls the woman in the extreme left foreground of no. 12, while the left-hand figure recalls Saint Lucy and one of the *Hortulanae* prints (no. 32).

The calligraphic signature is a more formal variation on

13

14

the simple name inscribed on the *Hortulanae* prints and the Magi. Technically this print has much in common with those plates and with the mature prints of the Holy Family (nos 6–9), particularly *The Annunciation*, which has a very similar use of stippling to evoke the paler shadows in the drapery.

14 *The Holy Women at the Sepulchre*

Etching and engraving. 438 × 289 (sheet trimmed inside platemark). Engraved inscription: *Bellange Eques incidit.* Watermark 18.

Walch 46 II. Worthen–Reed 62. Thuillier 32. Reed 191.

This subject – the *Visitatio Sepulchri* – was established in the Middle Ages as one of the earliest of the liturgical dramas performed during services at Easter. It derives from the passage in Mark's Gospel (16:1–8), the beginning of which was inscribed underneath Merian's copy of no. 13 (fig. 10). As in no. 13, Bellange does not show the women holding ointment jars, but his print follows quite closely the spirit, if not the letter, of Mark's description:

And very early in the morning the first day of the week, they came unto the sepulchre at the rising of the sun. And they said among themselves, Who shall roll us away the stone from the door of the sepulchre? And when they looked, they saw that the stone was rolled away: for it was very great. And entering into the sepulchre, they saw a young man sitting on the right side, clothed in a long white garment; and they were affrighted. And he saith unto them, Be not affrighted: Ye seek Jesus of Nazareth, which was crucified: he is risen; he is not here: behold the place where they laid him. But go your way, tell his disciples and Peter that he goeth before you into Galilee: there shall ye see him, as he said unto you. And they went out quickly, and fled from the sepulchre; for they trembled and were amazed…

Bellange shows the three women twice: once in the distance at the entrance to sepulchre; and then in the foreground, presumably inside the cave, confronted by the 'young man', who is represented instead as 'the angel of the Lord' (Matthew 28:2) sitting on the edge of the empty tomb. Bellange had already treated this subject in a composition engraved by Crispin de Passe in 1600–1601 (fig. 11; Hollstein 153). There the three women, holding ointment jars, are close by the tomb out of which pops the head, hand and wing of a much younger angel. The print completely lacks the drama of no. 14.

Worthen follows Walch in citing three engravings by or after Goltzius as the sources from which Bellange derived his composition, although these are partial and far from precise models: the angel is similar to that in *The Angel Announcing the Birth of Samson* (Bartsch 3); the right-hand figure is similar to one of the three women in *The Finding of Erichthonius* from the set of Ovid's *Metamorphoses* (Bartsch [anonymous after Goltzius] 62); and the arched entrance to the tomb is comparable to *The Resurrection* (Bartsch 38).

Perhaps more important, the organisation of the composition in terms of large dramatically lit figures shows the influence of Northern Mannerist prints, such as Aegidius Sadeler's *The Three Holy Women Visiting the Tomb* engraved after Bartholomeus Spranger (fig. 17; Hollstein 60), which has already been cited as a possible influence on no. 13, or Jacob Matham's *Diana's Nymphs Discovering Calisto's Pregnancy* after Cornelisz. (Bartsch 94).

As discussed in the Introduction (p. 29) the style and method of etching of this print seems relatively late compared to prints such as nos 10–12. An impression in Boston, which is one of only two recorded impressions of the first state (before inscription), is printed on paper with a crowned H, which was only introduced in April 1613 (see p. 130), so it can be reliably inferred that the print was made after this date; the same paper was used for early impressions of nos 9 and 12. As Worthen points out, Bellange appears here less interested in stippling and hatching for the sake of differentiating flesh from drapery: the neck of the right-hand figure melts seamlessly into the luminous form of her sleeve. Detailed description is sacrificed to effects of light and chiaroscuro.

15 *Pietà*

Etching and engraving. 309 × 196 (sheet trimmed to image, inside platemark). Engraved inscriptions: *Bellange Eques In. Incidebat* and *le Blond excud.*

Walch 17 II. Worthen–Reed 24. Thuillier 45. Reed 195.

The subject of the *Pietà* (in Italian: 'pity') – the sorrowing Virgin supporting the body of Christ after it had been taken down from the cross – does not derive from the Bible. It emerged first in Byzantine art around the twelfth century and became common in mystical literature of the thirteenth and fourteenth centuries. It was a popular subject in Renaissance art. The edicts of the Counter-Reformation censured depictions of the Lamentation over the dead Christ that showed the Virgin swooning in the arms of Saint John or accompanying angels, but Bellange has managed to combine the swooning and grieving Virgin within the same image. To some extent he has also incorporated the subject of the Crucifixion or Deposition by portraying the body of Christ in the position usually seen in depictions of those subjects, and elements of the Crucifixion are also made present by the inclusion in the bottom left-hand corner of the crown of thorns and a basket containing instruments of the Passion.

After the middle of the sixteenth century this type of *Pietà* almost inevitably reflected the influence of one of Michelangelo's famous versions. Bellange's version – his most monumental yet compact composition – has been compared by most writers with the presentation drawing that Michelangelo made for Vittoria Colonna, which was well known through sixteenth-century prints by Giulio Bonasone (fig. 28; Bartsch 64), Nicolas Beatrizet (Bartsch

le Blond excud

15

Fig. 28 Giulio Bonasone (active 1531–1574) after Michelangelo, *Pietà*, engraving 1546. 261 × 209 mm. British Museum

plate went through several states as the image was altered and improved, which again tends to contradict Thuillier's assumption that the print reproduces the resolved composition of a (hypothetical) painting. The changes are particularly apparent in the outline of Christ. The entire line of the right side has been adjusted and generally moved inward, thus altering his pose and making him a slimmer figure than that seen in the prints after Michelangelo, and one that is perhaps closer to Baroque art than to mid-sixteenth-century types. A similar tendency is found in some of Martin Freminet's paintings at Fontainebleau, notably *The Fall of the Rebel Angels* of 1608, but a more apt comparison for Bellange's Christ is the nude figure of Saint Sebastian in Aegidius Sadeler's print (fig. 29; Hollstein 95): both manifest the same febrile spiritual energy that animates Bellange's figure of the Virgin.

The alterations cause some uncertainty as to the exact distinction between Christ's right armpit and the drapery over the Virgin's knee. The altered contours have been over-bitten and therefore even in the richest of first-state impressions (such as that in Vienna) the emphatic and

25) and Agostino Carracci (Bartsch 103). Bonasone's print is the only one that includes the crown of thorns lying on the ground. The position of Bellange's figure of Christ in relation to the Virgin is similar to that found in these prints, although Bellange has omitted the angels that support Christ's arms. In addition, the shape of his body has been transformed so that his head is thrown back, echoing the Virgin's, instead of hanging limply forward. Whereas Michelangelo's Virgin holds her arms wide apart and looks questioningly up at heaven, Bellange shows her in a far more abandoned, swooning pose that recalls the ecstatic religious fervour of the visions described by Counter-Reformation figures such as Saint Philip Neri; these found later expression in Baroque manifestations such as Bernini's *Saint Teresa*.

As with many of Bellange's prints it is evident that the

Fig. 29 Aegidius Sadeler (*c*.1560–1629), *Saint Sebastian*, engraving. 455 × 325 mm. Fitzwilliam Museum, Cambridge

repeated outlines print rather inconsistently. As usual, stippling is almost exclusively reserved for the areas of flesh, with only a few touches on the Virgin's right sleeve. The plate was copied (in reverse) by Merian in a print that, in Thuillier's apt description, replaces the emotion of the original with a cold pathos. The comparison shows just how much of the powerful effect of Bellange's plate derives from the intensely personal nature and variety of the etched marks which he strived so hard to achieve. The stippling on Christ's flesh is not uniformly executed but is built up of etched dots and engraved flicks that each impart a different character of mark; the effect is then modulated with burnishing that adds yet another distinctive tone and texture.

The inscription up the right side of the plate is exactly the same as that on no. 16, which may have been published, and even conceived, at the same time, although there is nothing to confirm this in the rather incomplete evidence of the papers used for these two prints and, unlike no. 15, no. 16 never appeared in a later state with Le Blond's address added.

16 *The Raising of Lazarus*

Etching and engraving. 446 × 313 (sheet trimmed inside platemark). Engraved inscription: *Bellange Eques In. Incidebat.* Watermark 8.

Walch 47 (only state). Worthen–Reed 64. Thuillier 43b.

The story of the miracle of the Raising of Lazarus, brother of Martha and Mary, is told in Saint John's Gospel (11:38-45):

Jesus … cometh to the grave. It was a cave, and a stone lay upon it. Jesus said, Take ye away the stone. Martha, the sister of him that was dead, saith unto him, Lord, by this time he stinketh: for he hath been dead four days. Jesus saith unto her, Said I not unto thee, that, if thou wouldest believe, thou shouldest see the glory of God? Then they took away the stone from the place where the dead was laid. And Jesus lifted up his eyes, and said, Father, I thank thee that thou hast heard me. And I knew that thou hearest me always: but because of the people which stand by I said it, that they may believe that thou hast sent me. And when he thus had spoken, he cried with a loud voice, Lazarus, come forth. And he that was dead came forth, bound hand and foot with graveclothes: and his face was bound about with a napkin. Jesus saith unto them, Loose him, and let him go. Then many of the Jews which came to Mary, and had seen the things which Jesus did, believed on him.

As was common in art, Bellange shows the moment when the cloths are removed from Lazarus, causing those around to hold their noses or avert their faces from the stench. The two most prominent women are probably intended as Martha and Mary. The group on the right in the middle ground appear to represent the Holy Family with the infant Jesus. The naked figure seated on the raised ground looks at this group and seems to be drawing

their attention to the miracle in the foreground. He may represent John the Baptist in his role as the prophet of Christ's divinity and redemptive sacrifice ('Behold the Lamb of God, which taketh away the sin of the world.' John 2:29). The raising of Lazarus was often represented as a prophetic type of the Resurrection.

Most writers agree that the achievement of this print, both formally and technically, suggests that it is a late work, perhaps (according to Walch and Reed) Bellange's last plate, or at least the last of the large plates. This is one of the instances where Thuillier, in defining the late style of this plate, suggests that it prefigures the post-Mannerist styles prevalent in Paris in the 1620s and 1630s. While agreeing that the composition is more unified, the combinations of figure groups more fluid, than in nos 10–12, we cannot accept Thuillier's distinction between the figure style in this print and the group of Apostles that he dates earlier than the rest, but that we would prefer to define as late. In fact there are close correspondences between this plate and those Apostles. The figure of Christ, for instance, is not so far from no. 18, while the back views of the figures at left and right (particularly the former) recall no. 26 in their twisted bodies and crossed feet: hardly the choice of an artist seeking an escape from the extremities of such poses. Moreover, like certain of the Apostles, the main figures in no. 16 seem to exist in a convincing space, rather than being disposed on the surface of a crowded composition as was the case in the other large prints (nos 10–12).

Reed draws comparisons with several sixteenth-century versions of this popular subject, noting that it is closest in composition to Northern Mannerist types, although the comparison with Muller's engraving after Bloemart (Bartsch 27), suggested by Walch, only provides vague similarities. The smaller figures on the raised background seem to derive, with variations, from a pen-and-ink drawing in the Louvre (Thuillier 43a) that Bellange may have made in preparation for the print. The plate has the same engraved signature as no. 15, and it may well have been made at the same time: the treatment of Lazarus is particularly close to the rendering of Christ in that print. Unlike no. 15, this plate is not known in a later state with Le Blond's address, so although the inscriptions were probably added at the same time, the two plates were presumably separated early on in their history. As with several other plates, the margin at the bottom (trimmed off in this impression) remained blank.

Bellange Eques In Incidebat

17–28 Christ and the Apostles

All of the plates associated with the so-called 'set' of Christ and the Apostles are shown here, with the exception of *Saint Matthew*, which only exists in a unique impression in Berlin. The group is something of a puzzle on various counts. In effect there is a set of Christ, Saint Paul and the Twelve Apostles (four of them in two versions), who accompanied Christ on his ministry, with the usual exception of the traitor Judas Iscariot. Most sets of the twelve Apostles replace Judas with Saint Matthias who was voted as the replacement for Judas by the remaining Apostles after they had returned from Christ's Ascension. No. 27 is usually identified with Matthias, but it may well represent Jude who would otherwise be missing (see below). It appears that Bellange has replaced Matthias with Paul, who was appointed by Christ as Apostle to the Gentiles when he appeared to him in a vision on the road to Damascus. It may be that Bellange intended to add Matthias to his set, but there were certainly precedents excluding him: for instance, in the sets by Schongauer and Hans Baldung Matthias is replaced by Paul. Although the personnel of Bellange's set has usually been viewed as somewhat anomalous, it was normal to add Christ and one or two other figures to the set of original Apostles, usually the Virgin and/or Saint Paul: Lucas Cranach the Elder, Lucas van Leyden, Marcantonio Raimondi (after Raphael), Goltzius, Jacob de Gheyn (after Karel van Mander), Tempesta and Callot all include Paul and Matthias and most of them include Christ and sometimes also the Virgin.

The next problem is to explain why there are two versions of four of the Apostles: James the Greater, John, Philip and Thomas (nos 21–4). An examination of these figures suggests that Bellange worked on the Apostles over an extended period, during which he changed his mind both about the conception and the execution of the figures and so came to replace four of them. Two of the repetitions, *Saint James the Greater* (no. 21a) and *Saint Philip* (no. 23a), appear to be earlier in conception and execution than their replacements (nos 21b and 23b). Like the unique impression of *Saint Matthew* in Berlin (fig. 30, not exhibited) they are set against a blank background, whereas the other figures in the group have horizontal shading in the background. The prints with blank backgrounds also lack the stippling that is so deftly employed on the other figures. It is probable that these three plates are unfinished and would have been carried to a further stage of resolution, had not Bellange decided to replace them with very different figures when he came to complete the set. No doubt he would have gone on to make a second version of Matthew as well. Its survival in a unique impression suggests that the plate had already been reused or destroyed by the time of Bellange's death and was not therefore reprinted along with the rest of the plates in his studio.

Even allowing that these earlier versions may be

Fig. 30 Bellange, *Saint Matthew*, etching (Walch 30). 280 × 162 mm. Staatliche Museen zu Berlin, Kupferstichkabinett, Preussischer Kulturbesitz

unfinished, their conception is conspicuously different from their replacements. The figures are drawn with little suggestion of volume and with an emphasis on flat planes of drapery. In this they reflect Italian sixteenth-century models such as the Apostles by Parmigianino or Agostino Carracci. In execution they seem closer to Bellange's early prints, such as no. 4 (compare the face of James with that of Joseph), although what these mainly have in common is the comparative lack of finishing with stipple-work. The replacement figures (nos 21b and 23b) are startlingly different: elegantly turned, almost like Mannerist statuettes, with a slim serpentine grace and daring postures revealed through clinging drapery. *Saint James the Greater* (no. 21b) in particular shows the spiralling movement so typical of Mannerist sculpture, with a flame-shaped form emphasised by depicting the feet close together. The twisting is implied by the turn of the shoulders and the movement evident in the drapery; the 'first' version of *Saint James the Greater* (no. 21a) is by contrast very static. In the 'second' version of *Saint Philip* (no. 23b) patches of shading have been burnished and then strengthened with a burin, thus creating the shimmering light effect; the 'first' version (no. 23a) by comparison lacks the other-worldly quality conveyed by the use of light – it would appear earthbound if it was not for the halo, which is lacking in the 'second' version.

Now to turn to the repetitions where both versions have shaded backgrounds and there is not such a distinct difference of treatment. The 'first' version of *Saint Thomas* (no. 24a) shares something of the bulky drapery of the early versions of *Saint James the Greater* and *Saint Philip*. Bellange may have decided to replace it because of the ugly effect of the alteration to the head, but in any case his decision to etch an entirely new composition probably stemmed from the need to provide a more striking pose that would fit in better with the series as it developed. The 'first' version of *Saint John* (no. 22a) seems at first glance to be similar to the second (no. 22b), but an examination of the face shows that there is virtually no stippling. It therefore lacks finish in the same way as the face of Saint Anne in no. 4, and we may speculate that Bellange probably never finished the plate. Once more a technical deficiency – the unsuccessful attempt to burnish away the mark above the chalice – may have lead him to make a second version, but the decision to produce a different composition could have resulted from the realisation that the 'first' *Saint John* was rather too similar in pose to the second version of *Saint Philip*.

The Apostles in nos 21b, 22b, 23b, 24b and 25–8 exhibit the flame-like stylisation of highlight that seems to represent a later style. Thuillier sees this as an earlier style than that found in the prints with blank backgrounds (nos 21a and 23a), but we are convinced it is later, involving a far more sophisticated deployment of etching to achieve breathtaking effects of form and light. These prints are technically very eloquent, with a subtle flickering of stipple and, in the case of the 'second' version of John (no. 22b) and James the Lesser (no. 26), the use of brushed stop-out varnish to keep the shaded background lightly etched and set off the dark silhouette of the figure. The extraordinary depiction of the transition between neck and shoulder in Philip (no. 23b) is even more extreme in John (no. 22b), which is very similar in this respect to the right-hand figure in *The Holy Women at the Sepulchre* (no. 14). Thuillier interprets the lack of resolution and sophistication in nos 21a and 23a as a consciously simpler style that looks forward to the classicism of the 1620s; we prefer to see it as looking back to Italian sixteenth-century models. The later Apostles are far more personal in style and execution, and less dependent on the usual types found in earlier sets. A survey of sixteenth- and seventeenth-century sets of the Apostles reveals a tedious similarity of poses, gestures and iconography. Against this background Bellange's later figures are startling in their originality.

They take as their inspiration the extravagant postures found in single-figure costume prints by Goltzius and his school but not previously applied to such effect in prints of the Apostles. The closest comparison is perhaps with the series of Old Testament heroes, prophets and prophetesses after Goltzius (fig. 31; Bartsch 240–47).

Of the other prints, *Saint Andrew* (no. 20) seems closer in form and drapery to the early versions, particularly to *Saint Thomas* (no. 24a), and may well have been made relatively early in the set. It is closer to sixteenth-century types, such as Marcantonio's *Saint Thomas and Saint Paul* engraved after Raphael (Bartsch 72 and 76), than the later figures. The figures of *Saint Paul* and *Saint Peter* (nos 17 and 19) are more muscular and monumental in conception than the later group. It is possible that they were intended as a pair within the set, or even for separate issue, perhaps in combination with Christ; these two saints were often paired as joint founders of the Christian Church and placed on either side of Christ. The figure of *Christ* (no. 18) combines elements of this more monumental style with the elegance of the serpentine group. An alteration in the plate shows that Bellange made the form more flame-like by narrowing the drapery at the lower right: this was done after the background had been hatched and the patch of extra hatching to fill in the space is clearly discernible. The face is very similar in appearance and execution to the face of Christ in *The Raising of Lazarus* (no. 16). That print also provides a close comparison with *Saint James the Lesser* (no. 26): the figure in the left foreground seen from the rear, with crossed-feet pose and clinging drapery.

The Apostles represent the culmination of Bellange's interest in the manipulation of poses viewed from every angle, evident in his other sets of single figures, the Magi (nos 29a–31a) and the *Hortulanae* prints (nos 32–5). All three sets were executed on similar-sized plates. The Apostles are placed here in the order given in the Gospel of Saint Matthew and followed with little variation in the other Gospels as well as in the list at the start of the Acts of the Apostles. This sequence, which follows the order in which Christ enlisted his disciples, is followed fairly consistently in most of the sets of prints of Christ and the Apostles that were numbered. In his exploitation of the effect of viewing figures from different viewpoints (discussed under nos 29–31), the precise effect of the sequence of prints was probably a major factor in Bellange's development of the poses and replacement of some of the figures.

None of the prints is signed and the set was almost certainly left unfinished at Bellange's death. Early sets such as that in the Bibliothèque Nationale were probably printed soon afterwards, regardless of the fact that the plates as Bellange left them did not form a coherent group iconographically. Although no later publishers added their inscriptions, it is evident from the paper that the whole group was published later by Le Blond in Paris at the same time as those plates by Bellange that bear Le Blond's

Transfigens Sisaræ clauo caua tempora Jahel,
Æternum e tanto pectore nomen habet.

Quæ tua vis Sumson! quæ tantapotentia quiuit
vel maxilla asini sternere mille viros!

Dauid Gettheum strauit monstrum Allophylorum
Armatum a summo vertice ad vsqȝ pedes.

Aspice, quid potuit Judith præclara virago!
Quæ capnt in palmis en Holofernis habet.

Fig. 31
After Hendrick
Goltzius (1558–1617),
engraved by a
member of his school,
*Four Heroes and
Heroines of the Old
Testament (Jahal,
Sampson, David and
Judith),* engravings
*c.*1587. 267 × 167 mm.
British Museum

address (see p. 127). Certain of the prints appear to survive in greater number than the rest, and these are predictably the figures with greater individual appeal as votive images, such as *Christ* (no. 18), and the second version of *Saint James the Greater* (no. 21b) – a popular saint with a cult following.

17 *Saint Paul*

Etching. 283 × 161 (sheet trimmed inside platemark).

Walch 44 only state. Worthen–Reed 60. Thuillier 16.
Statens Museum, Copenhagen.

Paul is shown with his usual emblem, the sword with which he was beheaded outside the walls of Rome (he was entitled to swift execution by the sword – rather than crucifixion – due to the Roman citizenship that he inherited from his father). It also stands for the spirit and word of God as described in Paul's epistle to the Ephesians: 'And take the helmet of salvation, and the sword of the Spirit, which is the word of God: Praying always with all prayer and supplication in the Spirit, and watching thereunto with all perseverance and supplication for all saints.' (6:17–18.) Paul (formerly called Saul) was not one of the original Twelve Apostles. Indeed, he was involved in the persecution of Christians until he was converted to the Christian faith when Christ appeared to him in a vision on the road to Damascus (Acts 9:1–9). He was given the task of taking Christianity to the Gentiles. Bellange's representation is similar to that in Agostino Carracci's set of Apostles (Bartsch 62; the inscription on the print misidentifies the Apostle as Matthias).

18 *Christ*

Etching. 293 × 167 (sheet trimmed inside platemark).

Walch 45 (only state). Worthen–Reed 61. Thuillier 14.
Statens Museum, Copenhagen.

The usual devotional image of Christ. He raises one hand in benediction and in the other holds an orb (or globe) surmounted by a cross, one of the insignia of the Holy Roman Emperor and in this context symbolising Christ's role as *Salvator Mundi* – 'saviour of the world'.

19 *Saint Peter*

Etching. 293 × 165 (sheet trimmed inside platemark). Another impression faintly offset on the verso.

Walch 40 (only state). Worthen–Reed 56. Thuillier 15.
Statens Museum, Copenhagen.

The leader of the Apostles after Christ's Ascension and originally called Simon, he was given the name Peter ('rock') by Christ: 'Thou art Peter, and upon this rock will I build my Church; and the gates of hell shall not prevail against it. And I will give unto thee the keys of the kingdom of heaven.' (Matthew 16:18–19.) As was usual, he holds two keys, the gold key to heaven and the silver (or iron) key to hell; the book represents the teachings of the gospel that he was empowered to spread after Christ's Resurrection. Bellange follows the usual type of representation, but it is worth noting that he seems to distinguish the keys of heaven and hell by their place in the composition.

20 *Saint Andrew*

Etching. 280 × 162 (sheet trimmed inside platemark).

Walch 33 (only state). Worthen–Reed 49. Thuillier 17.
Statens Museum, Copenhagen.

Andrew was Peter's brother, and with him the first of the disciples to follow Christ. Little is told of him in the gospels and most of his iconography derives from later accounts of his life that were mainly known to the Renaissance through the *Golden Legend*. These tell how the wife of Egeas, the Roman governor of Patras in the Peloponnese, after being cured by Andrew, adopted Christianity and denied her husband his marital rights. Egeas therefore imprisoned Andrew and had him crucified on an X-shaped cross, which became his usual symbol. Bellange evidently altered the silhouette of the figure while working on the plate, for there is a trace of an earlier etched outline around the bottom edge and up the left side of the drapery outside the finished outline.

21a *Saint James the Greater* (first version?)

Etching. 281 × 163 (sheet trimmed inside platemark).
Watermark 2.

Walch 29 (only state). Worthen–Reed 45. Thuillier 18b.
Statens Museum, Copenhagen.

21b *Saint James the Greater* (second version?)

Etching and engraving. 289 × 167 (sheet trimmed inside platemark).

Walch 36 (only state). Worthen–Reed 52. Thuillier 18a.
Statens Museum, Copenhagen.

Brother of John (no. 22), and with him and Peter the closest of the disciples to Christ, he is called 'the Greater' to distinguish him from the other James (no. 26). He was the first of the Apostles to be martyred, being executed by Herod Agrippa in Jerusalem in AD 44. In the Middle Ages a cult grew up around the legend that he travelled to Spain to preach the gospel there. His body was supposedly taken to Galicia by his followers and in 814 it was claimed that his tomb had been discovered at Santiago de Compostela. Santiago (named after him, i.e. 'Sant Jago') became one of

17

18

19

20

the three main centres of Christian pilgrimage (with Rome and Jerusalem), and James is usually shown, as in both these prints, in the guise of a pilgrim, with a staff, a drinking-gourd (visible here only in the second version), and wearing his emblem – the scallop shell worn by pilgrims to Santiago (the origins of the scallop badge are obscure but it may have something to do with the fact that the scallop is one of the gastronomic delights of Galicia). The broad-brimmed pilgrim's hat worn by James in no. 21a has been sacrificed in no. 21b to the flame-like form of the figure.

22a Saint John (first version?)

Etching. 279 × 161 (sheet trimmed inside platemark).

Walch 43 (only state). Worthen–Reed 59. Thuillier 19b.
Statens Museum, Copenhagen.

22b Saint John (second version?)

Etching. 290 × 166 (sheet trimmed inside platemark).

Walch 41 (only state). Worthen–Reed 57. Thuillier 19a.
Statens Museum, Copenhagen.

Brother of James (see no. 21), John was later exiled to the island of Patmos and died at Ephesus. He is named as author of the Fourth Gospel, three biblical epistles and the book of Revelation (the Apocalypse). As one of the four Evangelists his symbol is an Eagle, but he is shown here with his usual attribute as an Apostle: a chalice from which a serpent emerges (or a dragon in the case of no. 22a). This derives from the legend that tells how Aristodemos, a priest of the temple of Diana at Ephesus, gave John a poisoned cup to drink as a test of the power of his faith. John made the sign of the cross over the cup and Satan flew out in the form of a dragon. John then drank the contents unharmed thereby restoring to life two condemned men who had died earlier from drinking the poison. In making his two versions Bellange kept the form and decoration of the chalice identical, but in the 'second' version (no. 22b) not only did he change the depiction of the devil from a dragon to a serpent (the Latin word *draco* can mean either), but the saint seems to be in the act of making the sign over the chalice with his hand, rather than merely holding it as a symbol. Bellange evidently took considerable trouble over this hand, as remnants of altered fingers are still clearly visible.

23a Saint Philip (first version?)

Etching. 281 × 162 (sheet trimmed inside platemark).
Watermark 2.

Walch 31 (only state). Worthen–Reed 47. Thuillier 20b.
Statens Museum, Copenhagen.

23b Saint Philip (second version?)

Etching and engraving. 286 × 162 (sheet trimmed inside platemark: image cropped especially at top and right).

Walch 42 (only state). Worthen–Reed 58. Thuillier 20a.
Statens Museum, Copenhagen.

Philip was one of the first disciples. He may have preached in Phrygia and was crucified at Hierapolis (according to at least one account, he was suspended by the neck to a tall pillar). His usual attribute, the tall cross, refers not only to the instrument of his martyrdom, but also to the legend that with the aid of the cross he banished a serpent or dragon that was being worshipped in the temple of Mars in Hierapolis. When the serpent emerged, it let off a smell so foul that many people died, leading the priests of the temple to capture Philip and crucify him.

24a Saint Thomas (first version?)

Etching. 284 × 164 (sheet trimmed inside platemark).
Watermark 2.

Walch 34 (only state). Worthen–Reed 50. Thuillier 22b.
Statens Museum, Copenhagen.

24b Saint Thomas (second version?)

Etching. 283 × 162 (sheet trimmed inside platemark).

Walch 35 (only state). Worthen–Reed 51. Thuillier 22a.
Statens Museum, Copenhagen.

Thomas, also called Didymus ('twin'), is the Apostle who doubted the Resurrection until he touched Christ's wound. As an Apostle, he is usually represented with a spear, the supposed instrument of his martyrdom, although he is sometimes shown holding the set-square of an architect or builder. Bellange's Thomas is very unusual in having a pair of compasses, or dividers, instead of a square, although these were also common symbols of the architect, especially in portraits. The association with architects derived from the legend told in a fourth-century apocryphal romance recounting the Apostle's missionary journey to India. King Gundaphorus ordered him to design and build a palace, but in the king's absence Thomas converted many of the populace to Christianity and distributed to the poor all the money intended for the palace. When the king returned, Thomas told him that he would not see the palace until after his death, because it was built in paradise; the truth of this was confirmed by a dead brother of the king who suddenly came back to life and said that he had seen the palace in heaven. Gundaphorus was immediately converted to Christianity. Thomas is the patron saint of architects and builders (although not specifically of builders' excuses...). Bellange's alteration to the plate in no. 24a, which shortens the hair and tilts the halo, is discussed above (p. 82).

21a

21b

22a

22b

23a

23b

24a

24b

25 *Saint Bartholomew*

Etching. 293 × 167 (sheet trimmed inside platemark).
Watermark 2.

Walch 32 (only state). Worthen–Reed 48. Thuillier 21.
Statens Museum, Copenhagen.

Bartholomew is only mentioned by name in the Gospels, although he may be identical with Nathanael who was brought to Christ by Philip (John 1:45–51). The *Golden Legend* tells of his missions to India and to Armenia where he was supposedly martyred by being skinned alive. As an Apostle, he is usually shown with the knife used for his flaying.

26 *Saint James the Lesser* (or *Saint Jude*)

Etching and engraving. 283 × 163 (sheet trimmed inside platemark).

Walch 39 (only state). Worthen–Reed 55. Thuillier 23.
Reed 188.
Statens Museum, Copenhagen.

James is usually identified with James 'the Lord's brother'. This gave rise to the tradition in art that James should be given features resembling those of Christ: Bellange does not give us the chance to judge! James presided over the Christian community in Jerusalem and was martyred there. An early source tells that he was thrown from the pinnacle of the Temple and then stoned or beaten to death, after he had refused to dissuade the assembled crowd from Christianity. The *Golden Legend* adds the detail that one of the populace 'laying hold of a fulling stock, dealt Saint James a blow on the head which spilt his brains upon the pavement'. James is therefore usually shown holding a club or fuller's staff. The alternative identification for this figure is Jude, who according to some accounts was also martyred with a club (see no. 27).

Bellange evidently changed his mind over whether or not to extend the drapery to fill the gap to the left of the ankles. The diagonal hatching in this area is not consistent with the horizontal hatching of the rest of the background, and the fact that the lines of hatching continue into the drapery suggests that it was originally going to fill this gap.

27 *Saint Jude* (or *Saint Matthias*)

Etching. 297 × 166 (sheet trimmed inside platemark).
Watermark 2.

Walch 38 (only state). Worthen–Reed 54. Thuillier 25.
Statens Museum, Copenhagen.

Jude (also known as Thaddeus), as distinct from Judas Iscariot, is uncertainly identified as Jude, brother of James. Apocryphal sources say that he preached the Gospels in Pontus and Mesopotamia, and then with Simon (no. 28) in Persia, where they did battle with two sorcerers. According to various accounts, the instrument of Jude's martyrdom was a halberd (a staff with an axe-blade attached to it), club or lance, which gives rise to some confusion in his identification. Although this figure has previously been described as Matthias, who was either crucified or beheaded with an axe, it seems more likely that it is Jude, with the turban conveying the Persian association. If this identification is accepted then we might be more certain that no. 26 depicts James rather than Jude.

Other sets provide inconsistent evidence of the attributes of Jude and Matthias, and the situation is exacerbated by the indiscriminate allocation of attributes even in sets where the Apostles are named (Agostino Carracci is a particular culprit in this respect). In some cases both Jude and Matthias are depicted with an axe (Callot), although Matthias is alternatively shown with a sword (Goltzius, de Gheyn) or a spear (Marcantonio). Jude is most often shown with a club, but Bellange may well have been following a pattern seen in Marcantonio's named set of Apostles, which shows Jude with a halberd and Matthias with a sword, and otherwise distributes the attributes in a similar way to Bellange.

Jude is the patron saint of lost causes.

28 *Saint Simon*

Etching and engraving. 293 × 167 (sheet trimmed inside platemark). Watermark 2.

Walch 37 (only state). Worthen–Reed 53. Thuillier 24
Statens Museum, Copenhagen.

He was called Simon Zelotes ('the zealot'), and almost nothing is known about him except that he was said to have preached the gospels in Egypt and then with Jude in Persia, where they were supposed to have been martyred. According to the tradition followed by most artists, Simon was martyred by being sawn in half, and he is usually shown with a saw.

25

26

27

28

29–31 The Three Magi

29a *Balthasar*

Etching. 288 × 164 (sheet trimmed to image, inside platemark). Etched inscription: *Bellange*. Engraved inscription: *le Blond excud*. Mounted on an old (17th-century?) album page, an offset of no. 30a on the reverse.

Walch 26 II. Worthen–Reed 33. Thuillier 35.

30a *Melchior*

Etching. 303 × 166 (sheet trimmed inside platemark at left and right). Etched inscription: *Bellan*.

Walch 28 I. Worthen–Reed 35. Thuillier 36.

31a *Caspar*

Etching. 282 × 167 (sheet trimmed inside platemark). Etched inscription: *Bellange*. Mounted on an old (17th-century?) album page, an offset of Walch 18 (see no. 37) on the reverse.

Walch 27 I. Worthen–Reed 34. Thuillier 34.

To save confusion, the titles used here for Bellange's Three Magi are those proposed by Walch and adopted by all subsequent writers. They are based on the traditional iconography which identifies Caspar, bearer of gold, as the oldest king; Balthasar, bearer of frankincense, as the dark-skinned king; and Melchior, bearer of Myrrh, as the youngest king. However, as Bellange did not identify his figures by inscription, there is some uncertainty, not least because Merian's copies (nos 29b, 30b and 31b) are inscribed with different identifications that contradict the usual iconography. The Magi are not named in the Bible and the usual names probably first emerged only around the ninth century. The traditional significance attached to their gifts was that gold represented Christ's kingship, frankincense his divinity, and myrrh (used in embalming) foreshadowed his death.

Sets of separate figure-studies of the three Magi were rare, but the chance to portray exotic costume, which was such a feature of many paintings of the Adoration of the Magi, made these an excellent choice for the type of costume figure that was so popular in the early seventeenth century. Bellange's single-figure prints recall those of Goltzius, and the demand for such costume-prints continued well after Bellange's death, when it was satisfied by Abraham Bosse, Jacques Callot, Wenzel Hollar and, of course, by copies and reissues of Bellange's own plates.

It seems unnecessary to presume, as Thuillier does, that Bellange's Magi derive from a lost painting of the Adoration. They were evidently conceived as a set, with each figure presenting a different viewpoint from the last. In showing us front, three-quarter and back views, albeit of different figures, they recall two sets of prints by Jan Muller (Hollstein 77–9 and 82–4) that each show a sculpture by Adrian de Vries viewed from three different angles, as though it is being turned before the viewer or as though the viewer is circumambulating the sculpture. Something of the same effect is also evident in the *Hortulanae* set (nos 32–5) and in groupings of the Apostles (see nos 17–28), as well as in Bellange's multi-figure compositions, where poses are varied by turning the figures round. The faceless back view of no. 30a is very similar to the central figure in the woodcut of *c*.1508 by Urs Graf, *Eight Men in Conversation* (fig. 32; Hollstein p. 53, 27); Graf's figure is itself an enlarged version of a figure in a battle illustrating Sebastian Brant's edition of Virgil published in Strasbourg in 1502 (see Giulia Bartrum, *German Renaissance Prints 1490–1550*, British Museum exhibition catalogue, 1995, no. 218). Bellange's use of this rear view in a single-figure print recalls the daring of Goltzius's back view of the Farnese Hercules (Bartsch 143) and serves as something of a foil to the costumed splendour of the other two Magi. We cannot even see the gift he is bearing. This was evidently too much for Merian and his publisher when

Fig. 32 Urs Graf (*c*.1484–1529/30), *Eight Men in Conversation*, woodcut *c*.1508. 318 × 226 mm. British Museum

le Blond excud

30a

31a

31b

30b

they came to produce their copies after this set, so in no. 30b they substituted a copy of one of the Magi from Bellange's print of *The Adoration of the Magi* (no. 10). Even then Merian felt obliged to alter the face so that the profile was showing. He also extended the compositions so that the headdresses were not cut off by the edge of the plate, and he managed to take the edge off the strangeness of Bellange's conceptions: a comparison of the face of Balthasar (no. 29a) with Merian's copy (no. 29b) reveals the individual power of Bellange as an etcher.

The copies are also more generalised in draughtsmanship and more mechanical in deployment of hatching. In nos 29a and 31a Bellange's control of the nuances and inflexions of the etching needle is used to evoke a sumptuous array of textures. Multiple bitings must have been used to produce the variety of lines ranging from filigree greys of embroidered ornament to the densest black of the fur edgings (the pursuit of rich blacks produced foul-biting in some areas). The very elaborate form of signature is only found otherwise in *The Martyrdom of Saint Lucy* (no. 12) and the *Hortulanae* (nos 32–5; there is also a variant form in

no. 13). The format and type of costume-print reinforce the idea that the Magi and *Hortulanae* were made around the same time. All three of the Magi were published by Le Blond in Paris, although two of the exhibited prints are earlier states, printed before Le Blond's address was added to the plates (nos 30a and 31a). Nos 29a and 30a are mounted on sheets from an early album that contained a sequence of prints by Bellange in a mixture of Le Blond and pre-Le Blond editions: other sheets from the album are in the Fitzwilliam Museum (Walch 7 III), Baltimore (Walch 18 II) and Washington (Bartsch 21 II). (This group is described and illustrated in the catalogue of the sale of old master prints, Sotheby's, London, 29 June 1987, nos 110–115.)

29b

MATTHAEUS MERIAN (1593–1650)

29b *Caspar*

(reverse copy after *Balthasar*, no. 29a)

Etching. 289 × 185 (plate), 326 × 211 (paper). Engraved inscription: *Caspar Rex Tarsis / Bellange. in:*

Wüthrich 86.

MATTHAEUS MERIAN (1593–1650)

30b *Balthasar*

(reverse copy after one of the Magi in no. 10)

Etching. 282 × 181 (plate), 307 × 203 (paper). *Baltasar Rex Saba / Bellange inventor:*

Wüthrich 87.

MATTHAEUS MERIAN (1593–1650)

31b *Melchior*

(reverse copy after *Caspar*, no. 31a)

Etching. 290 × 187 (plate), 321 × 208 (paper). Engraved inscription: *Tres Magi / Melchior Rex Nubia / Bellange invent: Jac: ab Heydé excu. / Argentinæ.*

Wüthrich 85.

32–5 *Hortulanae* (Gardeners)

32 *Hortulana*

Etching and engraving with drypoint. 306 × 168 (sheet trimmed inside platemark). Etched inscription: *Bellange* (lower right), *Hortulana* (near the legs). Engraved inscription: *le Blond excud.* Watermark 2.

Walch 14 III. Worthen–Reed 18. Thuillier 107. Reed 183. Statens Museum, Copenhagen.

33 *Gardener with a Basket on her Arm*

Etching and engraving. 287 × 167 (plate), 303 × 179 (paper). Etched inscription: *Bel. f.* Engraved inscription: *le Blond excud.* Watermark 2.

Walch 12 II. Worthen–Reed 16. Thuillier 109. Reed 185.

34 *Gardener with an Ornate Basin*

Etching. 313 × 166 (sheet trimmed to image, inside platemark). Etched inscription: *Bellange f.* Engraved inscription: *le Blond excud.*

Walch 13 II. Worthen–Reed 17. Thuillier 108. Reed 184. Statens Museum, Copenhagen.

35 *Gardener with Urn and Reticule*

Etching. 355 × 213 (sheet trimmed inside platemark at bottom). Etched inscription: *Bellange.* Watermark 1.

Walch 11 I. Worthen–Reed 15. Thuillier 110b.

These four plates are usually grouped as a set of four female gardeners (*Hortulanae*), the identification deriving from the Latin inscription on no. 32. However, no. 35 does not fit comfortably with the other three, being taller in format, rather stiffer and taller in figure-type, and etched in a different manner with rather less stippling on the flesh. It is also very similar in pose to no. 34, probably too similar for both to have been part of the same set. A drawing in Stockholm, apparently made in preparation for no. 35, has an alteration that changes the hand from the position seen in no. 32, possibly in an attempt to make the two etchings

Hortulana

le Blond excud.

32

le Blond excud.

Bol f.

33

Bellange ſ

le Blond excud

35

more different (see Thuillier 110a). Whether nos 32–4 were actually intended as a set of three is open to question (they are not exactly the same size, for instance), but they do form a coherent group of three in terms of their subject matter, their style and their varied but complementary poses. Indeed, the way they function as a group of three is comparable to the set of the Three Magi (nos 29a–31a), which are close in size. A drawing in Saint Petersburg (Thuillier 111) shows a female 'gardener' seen from the back, suggesting that Bellange may have been considering a *Hortulana* equivalent to the rear view of no. 30a (or no. 26).

The suggestion that no. 32 was intended as the 'title-piece', and that the omission of the title on the others was no oversight, is supported by the fact that the unique proof of the first state of no. 32 in Boston shows the inscription *Hortulana* etched by Bellange on the plate before he had finished work on the figure. The first state lacks some engraved shading and stippling as well as the burnishing of accidental marks around the outline, and the strengthening of the inscription in drypoint. There is also some adjustment of the fingers in the second state, and alterations to the hand holding the snake can still be discerned in this third state. Although nos 33 and 34 vary slightly in how many bitings in the acid they received, the group is coherent in technique and less complex as a group than the Three Magi. Generally the *Hortulanae* are more lightly etched and have less differentiation of mark through differential lengths of biting. Given that the two sets are very similar in format and style of signature (which they share with *The Martyrdom of Saint Lucy*; the abbreviated signature on no. 33 seems to have been altered from a fuller form), it seems that the differences reflect the contrast of subject matter rather than different stages of a developing style. The effect is much lighter, entirely appropriate to the lighter theme but also a result of matching technique to the need to depict lighter, plainer-textured draperies.

If we can judge from Callot's etching (fig. 5; Lieure 566) showing the appearance of the garden at the ducal palace in Nancy in 1625 (with some fanciful architectural additions), female figures carrying baskets on their heads were a real presence in the garden. Prints of gardeners were not uncommon in the late sixteenth and early seventeenth centuries among sets representing different trades and occupations. Bellange's figures derive from this tradition but are several steps removed from the usual appearance of such prints. There is some attempt to suggest realistic peasant-types, but their classical-looking sandals, which recall those worn by a very similar figure in *The Martyrdom of Saint Lucy* (no. 12), and their elaborate burdens evoke the world of court masques and playful garden sculpture. Although several writers have attempted to link them directly with pieces of court theatre, the prints are unlikely to be related to any specific event. Pariset suggested that they were connected with the Ballet des Bergères performed at the court at 1614, although the scant records concerning the ballet do not mention Bellange

(F.-G. Pariset, 'Dessins de costumes de théâtre de Jacques de Bellange et de l'Ecole Lorrain', *Revue d'Histoire du Théâtre*, 1954, p. 60). It has also been suggested that Bellange's figures were associated with the festivities held on the occasion of the opening of the new Italianate garden completed at the ducal palace in Nancy around 1611, but again there is no direct evidence. The same is true of garden sculpture, for although the figures do bear some relation to the fanciful sculptures of peasants scattered around the Medici gardens in Florence, the Nancy garden was apparently too formal for such casual conceits to be incorporated.

The designs of the four prints, all of which appeared in editions by Le Blond, proved popular. Merian made copies of all four (published by von der Heyden in Strasbourg), and these in turn were copied by the young Abraham Bosse in 1622. Merian's copies added landscapes, subsidiary figures and amorous Latin verses; the same title was used for the set, but it appeared on the copy of no. 33 instead of 32. But despite the adjustments, they remain essentially *gravures de mode*, or 'costume-pieces', and were evidently collected as such (see fig. 20).

36–7 Hurdy-Gurdy Players

36 *Blind Hurdy-Gurdy Player*

Etching and engraving. 295 × 175 (sheet trimmed inside platemark). Etched inscription: *Bellange. fecit.* Watermark 1.

Walch 21 I. Worthen–Reed 27. Thuillier 82.

37a *Hurdy-Gurdy Player Attacking a Pilgrim*
state I

Etching and engraving with drypoint. 310 × 210 (sheet trimmed inside platemark). Etched inscription: *Bellange feci* (trimmed). Watermark 1.

Walch 18 I. Worthen–Reed 26. Thuillier 83. Reed 192.

37b *Hurdy-Gurdy Player Attacking a Pilgrim*
state II

Etching and engraving with drypoint. 321 × 217 (plate), 343 × 231 (paper). Etched inscription: *Bellange fecit* (t on borderline). Engraved inscription: *le Blond excud.* Watermark 2.

Walch 18 II. Worthen–Reed 26. Thuillier 83. Reed 192.

These two subjects are the only prints by Bellange in a realist style, or genre. Elements of artifice remain in the treatment of the costume, but the unsparing depiction of the face in no. 36, and the explicit aggression of no. 37, seem to bring us close to the reality of life on the streets of seventeenth-century Nancy. The pilgrim in no. 37 is

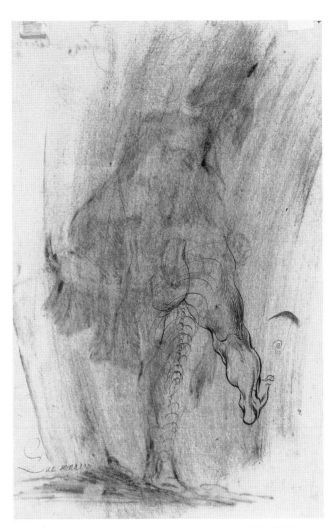

Fig. 33 Bellange (attributed), *A Blind Hurdy-Gurdy Player*, pen and brown ink over graphite. 295 × 191 mm. Private collection

Fig. 34 Bellange (attributed), *Buttocks and Leg of a Male Nude*, pen and brown ink (verso of fig. 33). Private collection

wearing the cockle-shell of Saint James (see no. 21), which had become a more general badge for pilgrims. It has been suggested by Reed that he is holding a recorder and that the print may actually show two musicians in a brawl. But it is certainly a pilgrim's staff and it is plausible that the pilgrim is only defending himself against the hurdy-gurdy player's aggression. We know that there were crowds of pilgrims in Nancy during the period in which Bellange made this print (see p. 31 above).

Both prints stem from a tradition of depicting beggars (occasionally fighting) and hurdy-gurdy players. In the sixteenth century they tended to appear in a moralising context, such as Bruegel's painting of the parable of *The Blind Leading the Blind*. Goltzius's engraving of 1586 on the same theme (Hollstein 111) derives in part from Pieter van der Heyden's engraving after Hieronymous Bosch (Hollstein 20); both depict a blind pilgrim carrying a hurdy gurdy and leading another blind pilgrim into a ditch. The hurdy gurdy was evidently associated with beggars, and

in particular blind beggars, who made their living by playing in the street. The continuing prominence of blind hurdy-gurdy players in paintings by Georges de la Tour, etchings by Jacques Callot and a plate previously attributed to Bellange (see Nancy 1993, nos 86 and 94–7) not only confirms the presence of such figures on the streets of Nancy but also hints at the likely popularity of Bellange's prints. Both appeared in later editions published in Paris by Le Blond (see no. 37b), and both were copied by Merian in prints issued in Strasbourg by Jacob von der Heyden. Merian's copies have moralising inscriptions added. In the case of no. 36 the German inscription is a somewhat lame jest with scant relevance to the print: 'A blind man, a poor man, it is said: Poorer he who is persecuted by his wife.' The Latin inscription added to the copy of no. 37, *Mendicus mendico invidet* (beggar envies beggar), surely comes closer to the message of brutal futility in Bellange's print.

The power of these prints derives from their immediacy, but each achieves its effect in different, artful ways. The

fiellange fecit

36

37a

37b

carefully contrived turmoil of limbs in no. 37 is brought sharply forward by the cropping of the hurdy-gurdy player at the right, the dog at the bottom and the pilgrim's staff at the top. The immediacy of the depiction is amplified by the acute rendering of textures: the deft combination of stippling and flecks that differentiate the coarse skin of the people from the matted coat of the dog. The subtlety of the etching in passages such as the pilgrim's bare knee is emphasised when one compares the tonal nuance of the first-state impression (no. 37a) with the second state (no. 37b). Typical of Le Blond impressions, the second state is harder in tonality, cleanly wiped and lacking in the delicate mid-tones. An impression in Nancy is inscribed in pen and ink with the date 1614, which may well be an accurate date for the print (Merian's copies are usually dated to 1615).

No. 36 is a different type of print, lacking narrative and concentrating on a single figure in the same way as the Apostles, the Three Magi and the *Hortulanae* (nos 17–35), which are etched on similar-sized plates. It is particularly comparable to certain of the Apostles, except that the gruesome face is less caricatured than, for example, *Saint Thomas* (no. 24b), while the luminous treatment of the drapery relies more on the optical effect of stippling than does *Saint Philip* (no. 23b). The detail of the face is an elaborate construction from stippled dots, delicately etched lines and flicks of the burin. The lines of ornament on the hurdy gurdy are also delicately etched, while the cross-hatching in the drapery has been etched for a much longer period. The darkest individual accents are made with the burin, partly to adjust the shading, but also to increase the sense of the rough texture of the cloth. Areas of highlight have been polished with a burnisher so that the plate leaves no ink on the paper and the boundaries of the shaded areas are softened.

A drawing in a private collection in England, reproduced here as fig. 33, has been attributed to Bellange. It is in pen and brown ink over an underdrawing in graphite. The outlines have been incised, and chalk rubbed on the back, in order to transfer it (there is also a partial drawing of the back of a standing male nude on the *verso*: fig. 34). It cannot have been transferred directly to the plate for the print, because there are too many differences between them, and the image is not reversed. However, it may be that this drawing was transferred to another sheet where the image was developed further, and then reversed onto the plate. Pariset suggested that the partially legible inscription – *Jehan de laroux* (?) – may be the name of the hurdy-gurdy player (F.-G. Pariset, 'Bellange et Lagneau ou le maniérisme et le réalisme en France après 1600', *Studies in Western Art*, vol. III, Princeton 1966, p. 124). Opinion has been divided over the attribution of the drawing, but the proposal by Comer that it may be a nineteenth-century forgery can certainly be discounted (Christopher Duran Comer, *Studies in Lorraine Art, ca.1580 – ca.1625*, PhD dissertation, Princeton 1980, no. x31).

38 *Diana and the Hunter*

Etching and engraving. 472 × 204 (sheet trimmed within platemark). Engraved inscriptions: *Bellange* (within the image); *Gaudet amans nympha si raptor Agenore nata / Dum sua tergoribus per freta furla [furta] vehit / Qua mihi nunc Impleut [Impleunt] placidam solatia mentem / Dum mea sic humeros pulchra diana gravata [gravat]* (in lower margin). Watermark 3.

Walch 10 II/III. Worthen–Reed 11–12. Thuillier 114. Reed 186–7.

The Latin inscription in the lower margin reveals the thoughts of the hunter, who carries hunting nets over his arm, and it clearly identifies his burden as Diana, the chaste goddess of the hunt: 'Just as the loving abductor rejoices in the nymph Europa [daughter of Agenor] while he carries her off on his back through the raging sea, so now solace fills my happy mind while my beautiful Diana thus burdens my shoulders.' In the eighteenth century the hunter was sometimes supposed to be Adonis (C. H. De Heinecken, *Dictionnaire des Artistes dont nous avons des Estampes*, Leipzig 1788, p. 424), but he has been identified

Fig. 35 Giorgio Ghisi (1520–1582) after Luca Penni, *Diana and Orion*, engraving 1556. 367 × 256 mm. British Museum

as Orion by nearly all scholars since Robert-Dumesnil's catalogue was published in 1841 (A.-P.-F. Robert-Dumesnil, *Le Peintre-Graveur Français*, Paris 1835–71, vol. v, no. 36). The identification ostensibly seemed confirmed by an engraving made by Giorgio Ghisi in 1556 after a design by Luca Penni (fig. 35) that seems to show the same subject, and which must have influenced Bellange's print. Since Pierre-Jean Mariette (1694–1774), Ghisi's print has consistently been called *Diana and Orion*, although Mariette added: 'It could also be, as Rossi says in his catalogue [1677], an allegory representing the lover of the hunt carrying Diana on his shoulders.' ('Catalogue de l'oeuvre gravé des Ghisi', ed. Jean Adhemar, *Nouvelles de l'estampe*, 1968, p. 376.)

Recent scholars have thrown doubt on the identification of the figures in both prints, because no identified source mentions the giant hunter Orion carrying his beloved Diana on his shoulders (see Suzanne Boorsch in *The Engravings of Giorgio Ghisi*, The Metropolitan Museum of Art, New York, 1985, p. 93). Orion was blinded by Oenopion, King of Chios, in punishment for raping his daughter Merope. He was told that the rays of the sun would heal him, so he put Vulcan's apprentice Cedalion on his shoulders to guide him toward the east where his sight was restored (a painting by Poussin in New York shows this episode). Orion later fell in love with Diana, who accidentally killed him with an arrow and then set his image among the stars as the constellation Orion. If Bellange's print shows Orion, then it conflates the two stories, replacing Cedalion with Diana as his guide, and showing Orion's great dog Sirius beside him. The arrow held so prominently by Diana and pointing towards the hunter's heart would then be ambiguous: the arrow of love, but also the arrow that killed him. The argument that the hunter is not large enough to be the giant Orion does not take account of the fact that the artist would have to maintain some parity in scale between the figures so that the idea of their relationship remained plausible in human terms.

In Bellange's print the identification of the huntress with Diana is confirmed not only by the inscription but also by the crescent moon, Diana's symbol, which appears on the top of the arrow. In Ghisi's print, however, the arrows are still in the quiver, and the inscription identifies neither figure. In 1987 Karin Orchard, without reference to Bellange's print, proposed that Ghisi's print depicts Milanion the hunter, who shunned the company of women until he fell in love with Atalanta, the huntress and follower of Diana who cruelly shunned the attentions of men (K. Orchard, 'Motive zwischen Jagd und Liebe – Zwei Kupferstiche Giorgio Ghisis', *Idea: Jahrbuch der Hamburger Kunsthalle*, 1987, pp. 31–5). Orchard cites passages from Ovid's *Ars Amatoria*: 'Milanion, roaming the forest, kept bewailing his lot, and the girl's unkindness. She [Atalanta] made him carry hunting-nets on his back, he was forever spearing wild boars.' (II 187–90), 'Milanion

bore Atalanta's legs on his shoulders: nice legs should always be used in this way' (III 775–6); and she points out that, although this subject does not appear in Renaissance art, Milanion and Atalanta were discussed by humanist writers such as Erasmus as an example of the 'servitude of love'. This identification leaves room for doubt. It fails to account for the crucifix clearly visible in the distance in early impressions. More important in this context, the idea of Atalanta riding on Milanion's shoulders depends on the passage quoted from Ovid in which the writer is actually describing and recommending different sexual positions. Other ancient accounts merely describe Milanion carrying Atalanta's hunting gear (Sextus Propertius 1.1.9–14), or he is sometimes named instead of Hippomenes as the lover who won her hand by beating her in a running race.

Even if it were accepted that Ghisi's print shows Atalanta and Milanion, it is by no means certain that Bellange saw it in this way (in the 1570s the publisher Lafreri seems to have described Ghisi's plate as *Diana and Actaeon*!), nor that he intended the same subject in his own print. In a recent catalogue of the Baselitz collection the same interpretation is applied to Bellange's print, without any reference to Orion (Karin Orchard and Thomas Röske in Ger Luijten (ed.), *La Bella Maniera: Druckgraphik des Manierismus aus der Sammlung Georg Baselitz*, Bern-Berlin 1994, no. 92). The suggested title is *Diana/Atalanta and Milanion*, based on the supposition that Bellange and the anonymous author of the inscription combined the identities of the two huntresses, reflecting the confusion between them in mythological sources. This seems to be stretching the evidence of Bellange's print, and it underestimates the differences between that print and Ghisi's, not least in the inscription. Whereas Bellange's inscription implies that the hunter is a willing lover, Ghisi's inscription reads: 'Foolishly I had believed that I could live for long in the woods free from the prison of love. But that god who is able to confuse the mind of men wants me to love her, though I do not wish to, and carry her on my shoulders;' this more closely accords with the Renaissance idea of Milanion. Details in Ghisi's print that support an identification with Milanion, such as the victor's wreath, are missing from Bellange's. Thus the Ghisi more strongly suggests Milanion, while the Bellange leaves more room for an alternative interpretation.

As Orchard (1987) points out, the idea of a lover carrying his beloved on his shoulders was not specific to Milanion but seems to have become a stock image for devoted lovers driven to servility. Nonnos in his *Dionysiaca* (XVI.82–91) describes the plea of Dionysus (Bacchus) to Nicaia (another cruel virgin huntress intent on emulating Diana) in a passage that ends in strikingly similar terms to the inscription on Bellange's print:

Receive me as comrade in your hunting: and if you wish, I will shoulder myself the sweet burden of your stakes, myself your ankleboots and bow and arrows of Desire, myself I will do it – I need no Satyrs; did not Apollo himself in the woods lift Cyrene's nets? What harm, if I also manage the meshes? I do not think it hard to lift my Nicaia on my own shoulders. I do not set up to be better than my father; for he bore up Europa in the floods unwetted, a seafaring bull.

This is not to suggest a direct source for Bellange's image or inscription, but it does show the sort of text that Bellange had in mind.

Bellange's print is much narrower in format than Ghisi's, thereby concentrating more closely on the figures and excluding the landscape, the distant group of hunters in Phrygian caps, and the group of five dogs, rather just one, in the foreground. Interestingly, Bellange avoids the opportunity to portray the goddess as explicitly topless whereas Penni/Ghisi took full advantage. In Ghisi's print the goddess is a weighty (though pneumatic) burden, whereas Bellange's Diana is a buoyant, seemingly weightless creature. Indeed the vertical emphasis of Bellange's figure-group shares much in common with Mannerist sculptures, many of which, such as those by Giambologna and Adrian de Vries, had been reproduced in prints.

There is a unique unfinished proof impression of Bellange's print in the Bibliothèque Nationale in which the forms and shading are sketched out in a preliminary fashion: some of the forms, such as the faces, are indicated only in outline, some have a base layer of hatching or cross-hatching, while others, such as Diana's arms and the hunter's chest, have an initial swathe of stippling. The hunter's eyes lack irises (giving him an appropriately blind stare if he were Orion!). His hunting net does not extend much further down than Diana's foot, and the swirl of drapery to the side of his right knee is missing; these elements, which were added in this second state, were indicated on the proof in chalk and ink. Although extra stippling and a good deal of hatching were added in the second state, some of it with an engraving tool, a lightness of touch was preserved which is similar in spirit to the *Hortulanae* figures (nos 32–5). Indeed, some of the lines that appeared disconcertingly dark in the proof, such as the hunter's hair and the hair along Diana's outstretched arm, were burnished so that they appear lighter in the second state. Also added in this state were the 'signature' and the Latin inscription that were evidently provided by the same professional calligraphic engraver, presumably on Bellange's instructions. Thuillier and Reed have recently proposed that the pen-and-ink and wash drawing of a similar figure-group (without the dog) in the Pierpont Morgan Library is more likely connected with a separate project, but the similarities to the print suggest that it represents an early idea as originally proposed by Reed (Worthen–Reed 10). When he finalised the composition for the print, Bellange added more elements from Ghisi's engraving.

39 *Military Figures outside a City*

Etching and engraving. 287 × 228 (sheet trimmed within platemark). Engraved inscription: *Bellange Eques in incide*. Watermark 32.

Walch 19 (only state). Worthen–Reed 28. Thuillier 116.

One of two plates (see also no. 40) with a very similar engraved inscription (no impressions survive without the inscription). This, together with the fact that they were consistently printed in later editions on a group of papers, none of which were used for any of Bellange's other prints, suggests that these two plates remained together and separate from the rest. Although Thuillier presumes that the inscriptions were added by a publisher after Bellange's death, this may not have been the case. It was certainly not the case, as Thuillier suggests, that they were added in Paris, as the paper used for impressions of these plates bears watermarks indicating that they were published in Lorraine. We know that a certain number of plates most probably left Bellange's studio before his death, so these two are very likely candidates.

In the light of all this it may be no accident that both plates portray secular scenes, and it is tempting to trace a narrative in this print to complement the episode from Roman history portrayed in no. 40. However, no precise subject has yet been satisfactorily identified, and Worthen (in Worthen–Reed) and Thuillier conclude that it is more likely a 'capriccio', relating to the type of antique-costumed military subjects popular around 1600. Interpretations have ranged from the vague *Encampment Scene* (Walch) to attempts to associate it with a specific narrative, such as Judith and her servant in the camp of Holofernes, or an allegory of Mars and Bellona. Walch argues that the seated figure is more likely masculine than feminine. This led Worthen to try to trace the subject in a cycle of paintings executed by Ambroise Dubois for the Cabinet de la Reine at Fontainebleau in about 1605, depicting the story of Clorinda from Torquato Tasso's popular epic, *Gerusalemme liberata*, first published in 1581. Worthen points out that Bellange was likely to have seen the cycle on his trip to Paris in 1608. But although there are close similarities of pose between the standing and reclining figures and those in two of Dubois' paintings, these figures could equally have been adapted from other sources (various figures in Mannerist prints are quite close in pose: see Muller's figure of Perseus, fig. 27; Bartsch 69), and Bellange used them himself in other contexts (see below). In any case, as Worthen concludes, it is clear that Bellange has not illustrated a specific incident from Tasso, and if the print has a narrative content it must be sought elsewhere. Thuillier observes that the fact that the city in the background does not appear to be under siege seems to rule out an episode from either Tasso or from the Iliad.

The poses and relationship of the reclining figure and the standing soldier recall the figure of Saint Lucy and the soldier to the right of her in no. 12; indeed the figure here

Bellange Eques in incide.

almost seems as though he is in need of a step on which to position his left foot. A similar standing figure occurs in *The Carrying of the Cross* (no. 11a) where we also find a recurrence of the extraordinary hat worn by the figure on the left. The manner of etching is also very close to nos 11a and 12, particularly the hatching and burnished stippling of the standing figure, and the more lightly etched grey background. These prints were probably etched around the same time.

40 *The Death of Portia*

Etching. 248 × 183 (sheet trimmed within platemark). Engraved inscription: *Bellange Eques in incide*. Watermark 31.

Walch 6 (only state). Worthen–Reed 5. Thuillier 118.

Portia was the wife of Marcus Brutus, one of the assassins of Julius Caesar. According to Plutarch (46:53), when Portia heard news of Brutus's suicide she was so stricken with grief that she also killed herself by swallowing hot coals. Bellange shows her at the moment when grief persuaded her to take her life. Her hand is poised above the urn of coals, with the heat depicted by an almost cartoonlike deployment of lines emanating from the coals. A painting by Bellange of this subject was recorded in the inventory of Claude Deruet in Nancy in 1662: 'Une toile ou est représentée l'histoire de Porcie avalant des charbons ardents, d'environs trois pieds moins quatre doigts en quarré, ledit tableau peint par le feu Sr Bellange, estimé à vingt francs.' As other writers have pointed out (Thuillier, Worthen–Reed), it is possible that this subject may also have been among the six scenes from Roman history that Bellange was commissioned to paint with Jacques Danglus for Catherine of Bourbon's room in the ducal palace in Nancy: Portia would have been seen as a suitable role model for a loyal wife.

The fine stippling and burnishing on the face and the burnishing of highlights on the drapery reveal the mature etching style seen also in the group of prints of the Virgin and Child (nos 4–9), and, as in those prints, the elegance and attenuation of the figure recall Parmigianino. For the inscription and publishing history see no. 39.

Watermarks in the Paper of Bellange Etchings

Introduction

The serious study of watermarks began towards the end of the nineteenth century, and found its first great monument in Briquet's dictionary. But for decades the only way to record a watermark was to make a tracing of it. This, as anyone who has tried to do it knows, is very difficult for non-experts; it is easy to see a line that is not there or to miss a line completely. As a result, the published records and dictionaries are variable in quality and have to be treated with a certain caution. In the 1960s the situation changed when beta-radiography was first applied to the study of paper; this allows an accurate and complete photograph of a watermark to be made. Beta-radiography, however, has the drawback that it requires a radioactive source and long exposures, and so its practical application has been limited. It has not yet been used in the compilation of any dictionary, and relatively few specimens have been published.

In the past few years H. M. M. van Hugten in collaboration with T. Laurentius in Holland has developed a new form of 'soft' X-radiography that produces photographs that are usually as good as beta-radiography but at vastly greater speed. Only a few minutes are needed, making it practicable to take large numbers of photographs, and this is beginning to transform the study of the history of the print. At present only two such machines have been installed in major print rooms: the pioneering work has been done in the Rijksprentenkabinet in Amsterdam, and in 1994 a second machine was installed in the British Museum through the generosity of the Josefowitz family. No one has yet been able to remake a dictionary of watermarks with accurate photographs. But by photographing large numbers of impressions of the same prints by the same artist, it has been possible to work out their printing history. A team from the Rijksprentenkabinet has used this approach on the etchings of Rembrandt, and has combined its results with a file of beta-radiographs that had been built up in the National Gallery in Washington. The preliminary findings have been published in the *Bulletin van het Rijksmuseum*, XL 1993, pp. 353–84. Further work has been done in Amsterdam and London on the watermarks of the engravings of Jan Muller (see *Print Quarterly*, XI 1994, pp. 351–78). Also Jan-Piet Filedt Kok has published a set of X-radiographs of Lucas van Leyden watermarks in the *New Hollstein* series (1996). The following listing of Bellange's watermarks is the fourth such project so far published.

Underlying this approach are two reasonable assumptions. The first is that plates were printed in editions rather than by single impressions. Copper plates need to have their surfaces protected and be stored carefully if they are not to corrode; then the surface has to be cleaned and a few impressions taken before they print properly. So an artist or publisher would, if possible, save time by printing at one time as many impressions as he was likely to need in the foreseeable future. The second assumption is that each such run (or edition) was printed from a pile of sheets of paper from a single batch. Since a professional printer would work systematically and be as economical of paper as possible, the watermarks will appear in regular and predictable positions on every impression from the same edition.

Professor David Woodward has recently published *Catalogue of Watermarks in Italian Printed Maps c.1540–1600* (Chicago 1996) with 335 watermarks of maps, based on 1,200 radiographs, and has shown that both these assumptions are correct; the maps do come with standard watermarks in standard positions. Of course this will not be true of every impression of every plate. The very first ones taken while work on the plate was still in progress will not obey this pattern; the printer here would have used odd pieces of paper he found in the studio. But if a printer had to run off an edition, he would have laid in a batch of paper for the purpose. A similar conclusion has been reached in the study of Rembrandt's etchings. Impressions from the same plate are regularly found to come from a very limited number of paper stocks, corresponding to a limited number of printings (or editions) run off at different times during Rembrandt's lifetime or after his death.

The following tables are the first attempt to do the same for the etchings of Bellange. The first lists every watermark that has so far been recorded on impressions of Bellange's etchings; the second records all the watermarks found on each of his plates. To understand them, a few general explanations about paper and watermarks must be given.

All paper before the end of the eighteenth century was handmade in a large number of small mills set alongside streams or rivers whose water provided the power. The water-driven hammers pulped linen rags into their constituent fibres in water, thus making a thick soup. Into this the papermaker scooped his tray. This was made of interlocking wires: the vertical chainlines were set somewhere between 18 mm and 38 mm apart, while the horizontal wires were set much more thickly running between them. When the surplus water ran off between the wires, the linen fibres set into a sheet that was then turned out and pressed between felts to dry. When such sheets are

WATERMARKS IN THE PAPER OF BELLANGE ETCHINGS

held against the light, the pattern of the chainlines and wiremarks can easily be seen: this is because the paper is thinner along the lines since the wire prevented the fibres settling so thickly.

Watermarks were made by the manufacturer of the tray (a specialist trade); the designs were made from bent wires that were then attached to the wires of the tray. Such marks were specified by the owner of the papermill, and served to identify his products or to distinguish a certain size of paper. Since papermakers worked in pairs, one forming the tray while the other emptied it, it was necessary to have two trays in order to maintain the rhythm of work. Since trays were ordered in pairs, the watermarks were in theory identical. However, since each was handmade, there are always slight differences, thus creating what are known as 'twins'. Trays seem to have lasted at most four years, often much less, before they had to be replaced. During this time the wires of the watermarks often shifted position or were slightly damaged. It is therefore possible, at least in theory, to distinguish earlier from later sheets of paper from the same mould.

The sheets of paper formed in the trays were intended to be folded when being bound into books. For this reason watermarks were usually positioned in the centre of the left side of the tray; frequently a countermark was put in the centre of the right side. However, many times there was no countermark and sometimes no watermark either. There are also oddities of placing: in the case of watermarks 3 and 28 in the following list, both watermark and countermark were placed on the same side of the tray, one above the other.

Only Bellange's largest plates were printed on an entire sheet. The smaller prints used a half or quarter sheet, possibly less. Identification of the paper of the smaller prints is therefore difficult. A watermark and countermark will appear on separate prints, and it is often not clear whether they come from the same mould. One might assume that the question could be resolved by measuring the distances between the chainlines: if they are identical, the paper will be the same. But unfortunately the process of tray manufacture did not permit exact accuracy of the spacing of chainlines, and there are always slight variations and sometimes very wide ones. Thus in the following tables ranges are given for the spacing of chainlines, and even these must be treated with a certain caution as sheets shrink differently; much depends on whether the same part of the sheet is being measured, and some are difficult to measure accurately. So two papers with chainline measurements recorded as (say) 33/34 mm and 32/35 mm might come from the same mould, but they might not. However, two sheets of 22/24 mm and 28/30 mm could not possibly come from the same mould. It is for this negative reason that chainline measurements are often given for unwatermarked paper. When enough radiographs have been taken, it might be possible to

get precise measurements of entire sheets and hence map them from one side to the other. This would enable unwatermarked sheets to be ascribed with certainty to one mould or another. But this is far in advance of current possibilities, and has not been attempted here.

The study we have been able to make of Bellange's watermarks is incomplete. It is not yet possible to get radiographs or X-rays of most impressions in most collections, and many collections have not been examined at all. But our study does allow a few general conclusions.

1. There was never a single edition of all the plates. In other words Bellange never issued his prints as a complete collection for collectors to buy as an *oeuvre*. This explains why no print room has a uniform series that appears to have been formed in the distant past: even the largest groups in Paris and Boston are assemblages put together in the nineteenth century. Bellange prints that turn up on the market today are oddments found in miscellaneous collections or groups of unrelated material (as Richard Godfrey tells us).

2. The only datable paper used is the crowned H (wmk 17), made by Demenge Aubert in the Vosges from 1613. This is found only on very early impressions of three of Bellange's larger plates, *The Martyrdom of Saint Lucy* (Walch 16/w16), *The Annunciation* (w24) and *The Holy Women at the Sepulchre* (w46).

3. Apart from the crowned H, only two other distinctively Lorraine papers were ever used. One is the CC of Charles of Lorraine (wmk 29), which was used long after Charles' death: it is frequently found on impressions of Callot's etchings. The other are the varieties of posthorn with the cross of Lorraine (wmks 20–22).

4. Two etchings, *The Death of Portia* (w6) and *Military Figures outside a City* (w19), share a type of lettering that is found on no other prints by Bellange. They also share three, possibly four, watermarks that are found on no other print (wmks 29–32). This implies that these plates shared a printing history that differs from that of all the other Bellange plates.

5. Almost every print that bears Le Blond's address is on the same distinctive thick paper with a watermark of grapes with AB (wmk 2). This implies that Le Blond printed one very large edition of all the plates as soon as he acquired them, and hardly reprinted them at all thereafter.

6. The plates that ended in Le Blond's hands also share a common watermark in the impressions printed before Le Blond's address was added to the plate; this watermark, which we have named the 'standard' grapes (wmk 1), is found on no other plates. This implies that this group of plates had been previously published as a group. The watermark has also been found on an impression of Lallemand's etching of *The Beheading of Saint John the Baptist*. Since this plate was almost certainly made in Paris, there is

strong reason to think that the edition of Bellange's plates with the standard grapes was printed in Paris before Le Blond's, possibly by Le Blond himself before he added his address.

7. Most of the large plates have distinctive papers (and therefore distinctive printing histories). Three plates share watermark 18 (H with letters on a cross). These are *The Martyrdom of Saint Lucy* (w16), *Christ Carrying the Cross* (w23) and *The Holy Women at the Sepulchre* (w46). Since it is found on many good impressions of these plates, a large edition must have been printed at the same time.

8. Only a few surviving impressions can be proven to have been printed within Bellange's lifetime. They include all the surviving working proofs (see w7, w9, w10, w14, w24 and w25) and the prints on paper with the crowned H watermark (wmk 17) that was introduced in 1613. It is quite likely that the great majority of other surviving impressions were printed after his death. Judgements can only be based on printing quality. One likely exception is the thin unwatermarked paper with a 21/22mm chainline that is found on outstanding impressions of the Three Magi (w26–8), some of the *Hortulanae* (w11–14) and possibly some other prints.

9. Very few plates seem to have remained in production long after Bellange's death. The main exceptions are the three very large plates: *The Adoration of the Magi* (w20), *Christ Carrying the Cross* (w23) and *The Raising of Lazarus* (w47), as well as the small *Virgin and Child with Cradle* (w7).

10. The set of Apostles (w29–45) presents peculiar problems. Their rarity today would suggest that few were ever printed. Yet four and perhaps more watermarks can be found on the prints, and one of these is of the paper used for Le Blond's reprints (though none of the plates ever carries his address). The confusion is deepened by the fact that three of the papers have very similarly spaced chain-lines, and this makes it impossible to attach the counter-marks securely. Unfortunately we have been able to obtain very few radiographs of these prints, and so our conclusions are less reliable than we would wish.

11. A particular comment is needed on one late impression of *The Raising of Lazarus* (w47), now in a French private collection (we owe our radiograph of this to the courtesy of the owner and to the help of Arsène Bonafous-Murat). It is printed on the reverse of the same sheet of paper as an etching by Grimaldi, *Landscape with a Man Standing near Two Seated Men* (Bartsch XIX, p.115, no.53). This is in a later state with the address 'Daman excudit' in the bottom left corner (not mentioned by Bartsch). Daman is an obscure publisher whose address turns up on later impressions of the etchings of Biscaino and elsewhere. Recent scholars have guessed that he worked in Bologna. This print, however, suggests that he must have worked in Paris. The matter is put beyond doubt by a series of six etchings of Roman views by Perelle with Italian titles that bear the address 'Daman excudit avec privilege du Roy' (a set bound into an oblong album of Roman views in the Lugt collection in Paris). It is quite possible that many of Grimaldi's plates were made in Paris, where he was working for Cardinal Mazarin between 1648 and 1651.

Acknowledgements

This project has only been possible in the first place through the generosity of the Josefowitz family, who gave the necessary equipment to the British Museum in 1994. We have needed access to as many impressions as possible and thank Hubert Prouté in Paris and Sarah Hyde at the Courtauld Institute for letting us photograph some of their prints. Ger Luijten generously had a number of photographs made of the prints in Amsterdam, as did Roy Perkinson at the Museum of Fine Arts in Boston, Suzanne Boorsch in the Metropolitan Museum in New York and Carol Eggert in the National Gallery of Art in Washington. At Windsor we have had the help of Henrietta Ryan and Alan Donnithorne. In other collections, however, we have had to rely on our eyes, with all the errors that that entails. We thank all those who helped us, and particularly Maxime Préaud in the Réserve of the Bibliothèque Nationale, John Ittmann at the Philadelphia Museum of Art, and Catherine Bindman in the Metropolitan Museum. Robert Gerard examined for us the impressions in New York, and Jonathan Bober reported on a print in the Archer M. Huntington Art Gallery of the University of Texas at Austin. All the radiographs in the British Museum were taken by Janet Lang, whom we warmly thank.

Photographed Watermarks

The following list contains all the watermarks for which we have been able to obtain an X- or beta-radiograph, with a note of every impression on which we have found them. They are reproduced in the plates that follow. Some watermarks that we have noted but that we have not been able to photograph are recorded in the next section (pp. 135–40). There are doubtless many more that we have not seen.

References to the following standard dictionaries have been abbreviated as follows:

Briquet: C. M. Briquet, *Les Filigranes*, 4 vols, Geneva 1907 (the 1968 Amsterdam reprint includes an introduction by Allen Stevenson that serves as an excellent introduction to the study of watermarks)

Gaudriault: Raymond Gaudriault, *Filigranes et autres caractéristiques des papiers fabriqués en France aux XVIIe et XVIIIe siècles*, Paris 1995

Heawood: E. Heawood, *Watermarks Mainly of the XVII and XVIII Centuries*, Hilversum 1950

Janot: Jean-Marie Janot, *Les Moulins à papier de la région vosgienne*, Nancy 1952

Nicolai: Alexandre Nicolai, *Histoire des moulins à papier dans le sud-ouest de la France 1300–1800*, 2 vols, Bordeaux 1935

Wiener: Lucien Wiener, *Etude sur les filigranes des papiers Lorrains*, Nancy 1893

GRAPE WATERMARKS

1. 'Standard' grapes with stalk, 9 × 6 rows, 40 × 25 mm overall, on 20/22 mm chainline touching either side. This only appears on plates that later carry Le Blond's address. See p. 126, under point 6.

w9 I	*The Virgin and Child with Distaff and an Angel*
WII I	*Gardener with Urn and Reticule*
WI5 I	*The Holy Family with Saint Catherine and others*
w18 I	*Hurdy-Gurdy Player Attacking a Pilgrim*
W21 I	*Blind Hurdy-Gurdy Player*
w26 I	*Balthasar*
w27 I	*Caspar*
w28 I	*Melchior*
w (reject)	*The Holy Family with Mary Magdalene and Saint Anne*

2. 'Le Blond' grapes with AB mark above, 10 × 6 rows on 33/34 mm chainlines; cf. Briquet 13206 for grapes with a separate AB countermark, recorded at Lyons 1630. This paper seems to be used on all the Le Blond reissues. Illustrated are a pair of 'twins'. See p. 126.

W10 III	*Diana and the Hunter*
WII II	*Gardener with Urn and Reticule*
WI2 II	*Gardener with a Basket on her Arm*
WI3 II	*Gardener with an Ornate Basin*
WI4 III	*Hortulana*
WI5 II	*The Holy Family with Saint Catherine and others*
WI7 II	*Pietà*
WI8 II	*Hurdy-Gurdy Player Attacking a Pilgrim*
w26 II	*Balthasar*
w27 II	*Caspar*
w28 II	*Melchior*
w29, 31–45	Set of Apostles

3. Grapes, 11 × 6 rows, 31 × 20 mm overall, on 33/35 mm chainline + separate AIR countermark placed below on the same side of the sheet; cf. Heawood 2226/7 (other grapes with AIR countermark): found on 1620 Paris publications.

W10 II	*Diana and the Hunter*

4. AIR countermark to uncertain variety of grapes, on paper with chainlines 32/34mm, very similar to the above.

WI5 I	*The Holy Family with Saint Catherine and others*

5. Small grapes with stalk, 8 × 5 rows, 18 × 33 mm overall, on 34 mm chainlines + small AIR countermark (not illustrated) set vertically between the chainlines measuring 7 × 22 mm.

w29, 31–45	Set of Apostles
w36	*Saint James the Greater*

6a/b. AIR countermark found on impressions of the Apostles, on paper with 33/35 mm chainlines (2 variants); probably variations of the above or the following.

w36	*Saint James the Greater*
w38	*Saint Jude/Matthias*
w41	*Saint John*
w45	*Christ*

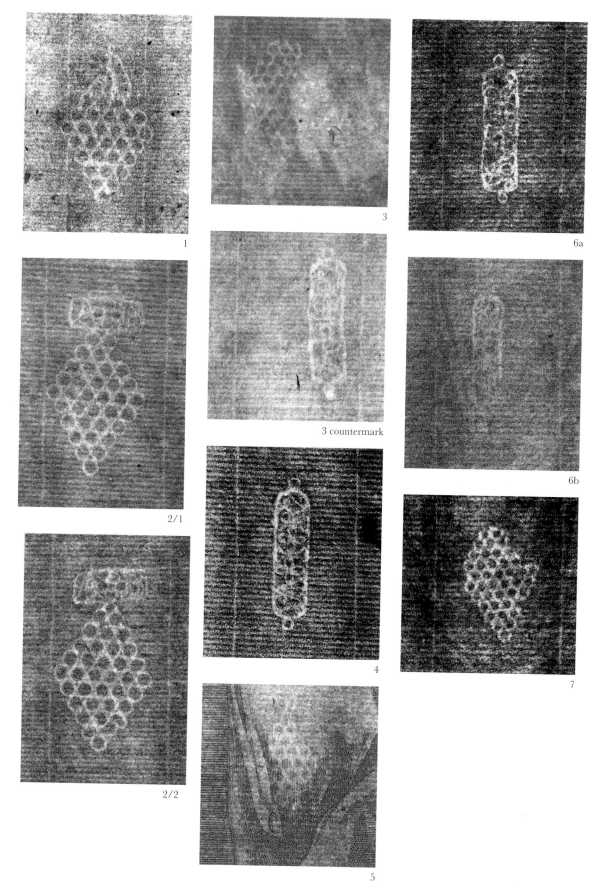

1

2/1

2/2

3

3 countermark

4

5

6a

6b

7

7. Grapes, 11 × 7 rows, on 33/34 mm chainlines.

    w44   *Saint Paul*

8. 'Molecule' grapes, 61 × 39 mm overall, on 24/27 mm chainlines.

    w 47   *The Raising of Lazarus*

9. Small grapes, 12 × 7 rows, 60 × 27 mm overall, on 30/32 mm chainlines.

    w20 II   *The Adoration of the Magi*

10. Small grapes, 12 × 7 rows, 49 × 25 mm overall, on 33/35 mm chainlines

    w12 I   *Gardener with a Basket on her Arm*

11. Large grapes with curving stalk, 9 × 6 rows, 47 × 27 mm overall, on 24/31 mm chainlines.

    w22   *Three Holy Women*

12. Grapes with CB and fleur-de-lys, on 21 mm chainlines; cf. Gaudriault 955 from Nicolai, II p. 94 and pl. 117, nos 3–4. Identified as the mark of C. Bardy, near Bordeaux, active *c.*1619. Variants Heawood 2329, 2335.

    w3   *The Vision of Saint Norbert in Prémontré*

13. Grapes, 5 × 8 rows, with CB above, on 21/22 mm chainlines + PD countermark.

    w24   *The Annunciation*

    w46 II   *The Holy Women at the Sepulchre*

14. Large grapes with BV in heart, 12 × 7 rows on 33/34 mm chainlines.

    w47   *The Raising of Lazarus*

15. Grapes in circle with COLONBIER round outside; cf. Heawood 2429: Auvergne paper of Benoît Colombier of 1650s/1660s.

    w47   *The Raising of Lazarus*

16. Variety of above.

    w47   *The Raising of Lazarus*

NON-GRAPE WATERMARKS

17. Crowned H + FA countermark on 22/24 mm chainlines. See Janot (Vosges), pp. 172–6. The mark of Demenge Aubert (son of Florentin) of Cheniménil in the Vosges, who petitioned Henri II to use this mark in April 1613 and was given sole rights to it.

    w16   *The Martyrdom of Saint Lucy*

    w24 I   *The Annunciation*

    w46 I   *The Holy Women at the Sepulchre*

18. H with letters on a cross, on 29/32 mm chainlines.

    w16   *The Martyrdom of Saint Lucy*

    w23   *Christ Carrying the Cross*

    w46 II   *The Holy Women at the Sepulchre*

19. Posthorn in a shield on 27 mm chainlines.

    w46 II   *The Holy Women at the Sepulchre*

20. Posthorn in a shield, on chainlines 28/29 mm.

    w16   *The Martyrdom of Saint Lucy*

21. Posthorn, on 22/27 mm chainlines.

    w9 I   *The Virgin and Child with Distaff and an Angel*

22a/b/c. Posthorn with Cross of Lorraine on 22/27 mm chainlines (3 variants).

    w24 II   *The Annunciation*

23. Fleur-de-lys on 28/30 mm chainlines.

    w23   *Christ Carrying the Cross*

24. Flower with AR on 37/38 mm chainlines.

    w23   *Christ Carrying the Cross*

25. Arms of France and Navarre (i.e. of Henri IV) in a shield with 'G. Journee', on 20/22 mm chainlines. See Le Clert (Troyes) nos 160–61. Mark of Guillaume Journée of Troyes, working 1594–1621.

    w7 I   *The Virgin and Child with Cradle (proof)*

26. Crown above shield with letter R, on 25/26 mm chainlines

    w8 I   *The Virgin Wrapping the Child in Swaddling Clothes*

27. Shield with crossed batons and fleur-de-lys, on 37/38 mm chainlines.

    w20 II   *The Adoration of the Magi*

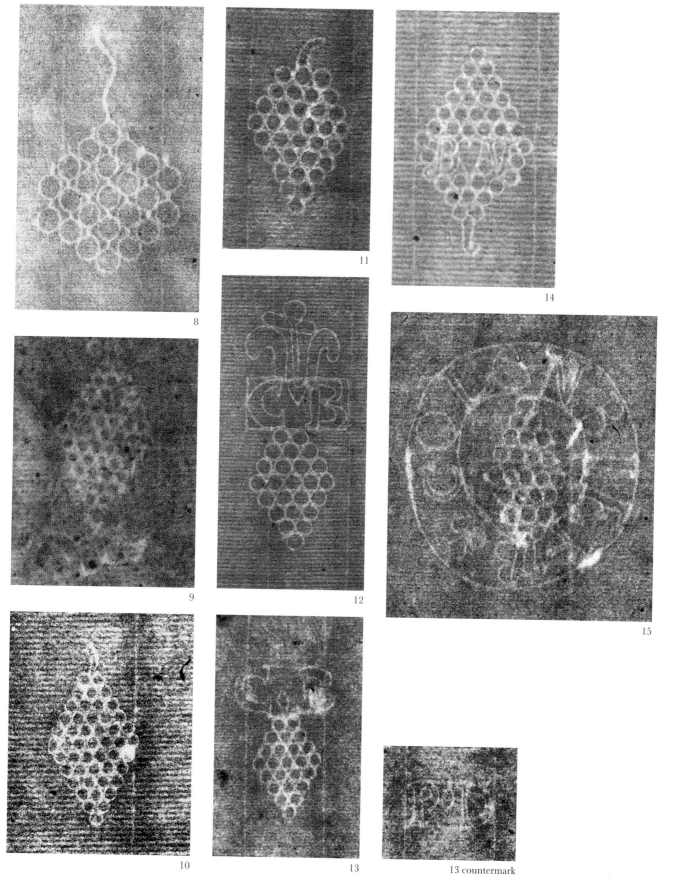

8

9

10

11

12

13

14

15

13 countermark

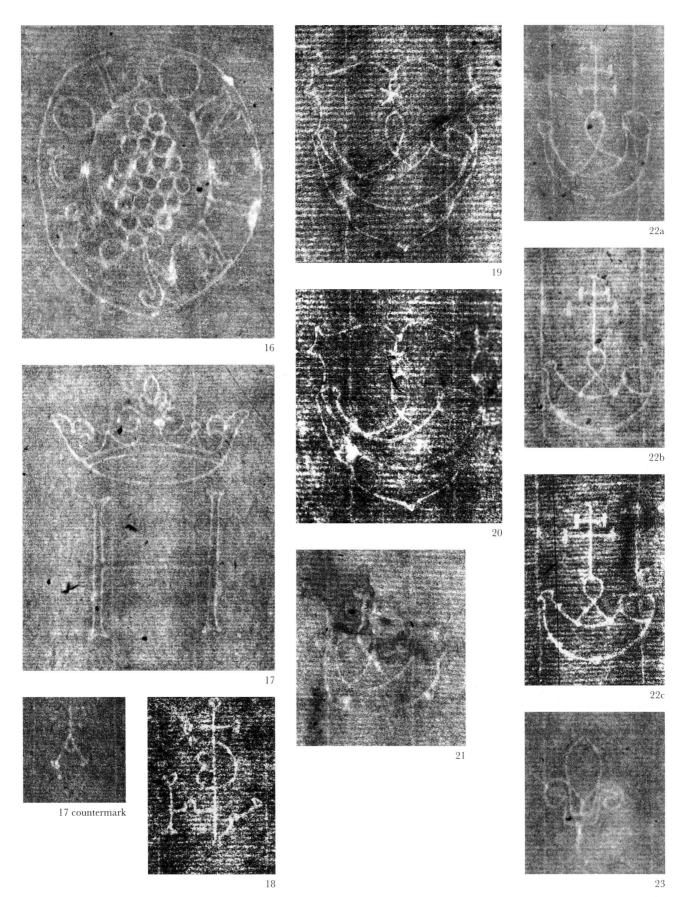

16

17

17 countermark

18

19

20

21

22a

22b

22c

23

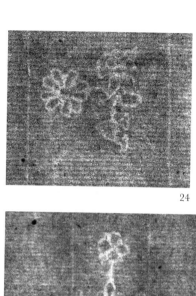

24

27

29

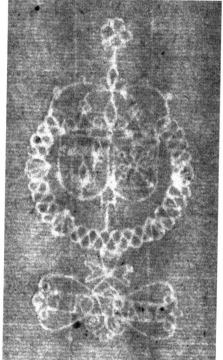

25

29 countermark

28 (reduced: original size 112 × 84mm)

26

28 countermark

30 countermark

30

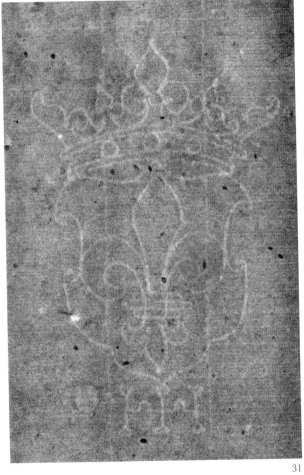

32

32 countermark

31

33 (photographed against the light)

28. Double-headed eagle + LEBLOYS countermark, on 34 mm chainlines; cf. Gaudriault 34, as 1690?

w20 v *The Adoration of the Magi*

29. CC + countermark on 22/24 mm chainlines; cf. Wiener pls 2, 3 and Gaudriault 529–35. The CC are for Charles III of Lorraine and his wife Claude de France. It was first used by Florentin Aubert but later widely copied.

w6   *The Death of Portia*

w19   *Military Figures outside a City*

30. Small eagle + arrow countermark on 22/24 mm chainlines.

w6   *The Death of Portia*

w19   *Military Figures outside a City* (very similar but not identical)

31. Fleur-de-lys in shield with HH below on 26/27 mm chainlines. See Heawood 1767, found at Frankfurt 1625. For HH, see Heawood 1286 and 1290, as Hans Hurnpain of Kempten, and dated 1622/4.

w6   *The Death of Portia*

32. Rampant lion + posthorn countermark on 21/23 mm chainlines.

w6   *Death of Portia*

w19   *Military Figures outside a City*

33. Shield with a line of letters on 21/22 mm chainlines. (This has been photographed using transmitted light, not by radiography.)

w11   *Hortulana*

Identified Watermarks Listed by Title

The following table lists every impression whose watermark has been photographed (that is all those in the Josefowitz collection and the British Museum, plus a few selected items in other collections) as well as most of the impressions that we have been able to examine elsewhere by eye. A few prints that we have seen but have defeated us are not mentioned. Cases where a substantial element of guesswork is involved are marked with an asterisk. A blank in the 'State' column means that only a single state is known. When unwatermarked paper is listed immediately after watermarked paper with the same chainline measurements, there is a good chance that it comes from the same paper stock. Conversely, when an unwatermarked paper is listed with chainlines that differ, it cannot come from the same stock. We have included some watermarks that we have seen but have not been able to photograph.

The watermarks are listed according to Walch numbers in what we judge to be the order of printing, based on the quality of impression. The numbers before the watermarks refer to those in the preceding list.

Key to collections

Amsterdam:	Rijksmuseum, Amsterdam
BM:	British Museum, London
BN:	Bibliothèque Nationale, Paris
Boston:	Museum of Fine Arts, Boston
Copenhagen:	Statens Museum for Kunst, Copenhagen
Courtauld:	Courtauld Institute of Art, London
Houston:	Museum of Fine Art, Houston
JC:	Josefowitz collection (the listing includes various duplicates that are not included in the exhibition)
MMA:	Metropolitan Museum of Art, New York
Munich:	Staatliche Graphische Sammlung, Munich
NYPL:	New York Public Library
Ottawa:	National Gallery of Canada, Ottawa
Oxford:	Ashmolean Museum, Oxford
Philadelphia:	Philadelphia Museum of Art
Prouté:	private collection of Hubert Prouté, Paris
Texas:	Archer M. Huntington Art Gallery, University of Texas at Austin
Washington:	National Gallery of Art, Washington
Windsor:	Royal Library, Windsor Castle

Walch No.	Title	State	Watermark	Location
W1	*The Entry of Henri II into Nancy*		nothing, chainlines 24/25mm	BM; JC
W3	*The Vision of Saint Norbert in Prémontré*		12: grapes with CB and fleur-de-lys	JC
			variant grapes with countermark, chainlines 23/24mm (no photo)	BN
W4	*The Virgin Bestowing a Scapular on a Monk*		nothing, chainlines 22/23mm	Philadelphia
W5	*Saint Augustine in Prayer*		nothing, chainlines 22/23mm	Boston
W6	*The Death of Portia*		29: CC + countermark	Amsterdam; JC
			30: eagle + arrow countermark	BM; Boston; BN*
			31: fleur-de-lys in shield with HH	JC
			32: rampant lion + posthorn countermark	MMA; Philadelphia
W7	*The Virgin and Child with Cradle*	I (unique working proof)	25: arms of France and Navarre	Courtauld
		II	nothing, chainlines 21/23mm	JC; Boston; BN*; Prouté*
		III (Le Blond)	nothing, chainlines 33/34mm	BM; Boston
		IV (post-Le Blond)	nothing, chainlines 23/26mm	Boston
W8	*The Virgin Wrapping the Child in Swaddling Clothes*	I (pre-Le Blond)	26: crown above shield with letter A	Boston
		II (Le Blond)	nothing, chainlines 33/34mm	BN; MMA (state uncertain)
W9	*The Virgin and Child with Distaff and an Angel*	I (before signature)	21: posthorn	Prouté
		II (with signature)	nothing, chainlines 21/22mm	Washington
			1: standard grapes	BM; BN; JC
		III (Le Blond)	2: grapes with AB	MMA
W10	*Diana and the Hunter*	I (unique working proof)	nothing, chainlines 25/26mm	BN
		II (pre-Le Blond)	3: grapes + AIR countermark on separate sheets	JC(grapes); Amsterdam (AIR)
			grapes with countermark B[?], chainlines 33/34mm (no photo)	BN
		III (Le Blond)	2: grapes with AB	JC; Copenhagen; MMA; Philadelphia
W11	*Gardener with Urn and Reticule*	I (pre-Le Blond)	nothing, chainlines 21mm	Prouté
			33: shield with line of text on 21/22mm	Munich
			1: standard grapes	JC
		II (Le Blond)	2: grapes with AB	Philadelphia
			nothing, chainlines 33/34mm	Boston (state uncertain)

Walch No.	Title	State	Watermark	Location
W12	*Gardener with a Basket on her Arm*	I (pre-Le Blond)	grapes in 15 rows with mark below, chainlines 19/20mm (no photo)	BN
			grapes, 16 × 9 rows, with quatrefoil below with initials(?) either side (cf. Gaudriault 949, 950), chainlines 19/21mm (no photo)	Philadelphia
			10: small 12 × 7 grapes, chainlines 21/22mm	MMA
			nothing, chainlines 21/22mm	BN; Amsterdam
		II (Le Blond)	2: grapes with AB	JC
			nothing, chainlines 33/34mm	BM; Copenhagen
W13	*Gardener with an Ornate Basin*	I (pre-Le Blond)	nothing, chainlines 21/22mm	BN(two); Amsterdam
			1: standard grapes	Boston*
		II (Le Blond)	2: grapes with AB	BM
			nothing, chainlines 33/34mm	Copenhagen; Philadelphia
W14	*Hortulana*	I (working proof)	nothing, chainlines 22/23mm	Boston
		II (pre-Le Blond)	nothing, chainlines 21/22mm	BN; Prouté; Amsterdam
		III (Le Blond)	2: grapes with AB	Copenhagen
W15	*The Holy Family with Saint Catherine, Saint John the Evangelist and an Angel*	I (pre-Le Blond)	nothing, chainlines 21/22mm	Copenhagen; MMA; Boston; BN*
			4: AIR countermark, chainlines 32/35mm	Amsterdam; BM
			1: standard grapes	JC; Philadelphia
		II (Le Blond)	2: grapes with AB	Boston
			nothing, chainlines 33/34mm	Prouté
W16	*The Martyrdom of Saint Lucy*		17: crowned H + FA	Prouté
			20: posthorn	Boston; BN*
			18: H with letters on cross	Amsterdam; BM; JC(two); Boston(two)
			nothing, chainlines 31/32mm	MMA
			nothing, chainlines 27/29mm	Washington
W17	*Pietà*	I (pre-Le Blond)	nothing, chainlines 20/22mm	BM; Boston; BN*
		II (Le Blond)	2: grapes with AB	Amsterdam; MMA
			nothing, chainlines 33/34mm	JC
W18	*Hurdy-Gurdy Player Attacking a Pilgrim*	I (pre-Le Blond)	1: standard grapes	BM; BN; JC; MMA; Boston*
			nothing, chainlines 21/22mm	Copenhagen; Amsterdam
		II (Le Blond)	2: grapes with AB	JC
W19	*Military Figures outside a City*		29: CC + countermark	BN*
			30: eagle + arrow countermark	Amsterdam
			31: rampant lion + posthorn countermark	BM; Prouté; MMA; JC; Boston; Philadelphia

(cf. W6: the order of printing is not certain. Worthen–Reed also record an impression with the arms of Dachsbourg, a shield with 8 batons, and refer to Wiener pl. 13, no. 7.)

Walch No.	Title	State	Watermark	Location
W20	*The Adoration of the Magi*	I (before signature)	crossed arrows (no photo; Briquet 6283)	Ottawa (recorded by Worthen–Reed)
		II (with signature)	9: small 12 × 7 grapes	JC; BN*
			nothing, chainlines 33/35mm	Houston
			27: shield, chainlines 37/38mm	Boston
		V (after van Merle)	28: double-headed eagle + LEBLOYS	Boston
W21	*Blind Hurdy-Gurdy Player*	I (pre-Le Blond)	1: standard grapes	JC; BN; Windsor
			nothing, chainlines 33/34mm	Boston
W22	*Three Holy Women*		nothing, chainlines 21/22mm	BM; JC(two); BN(two); Boston
			11: large 9x6 grapes	JC
			6 × 6 grapes, chainlines 26/28mm (no photo)	Prouté
W23	*Christ Carrying the Cross*		18: H with letters on cross	Prouté; BN; MMA; Boston*
			23: fleur-de-lys	JC
			24: flower with AR	JC
W24	*The Annunciation*	I (before signature)	17: crowned H + FA countermark	Boston
		II (with signature)	22a/b/c: posthorn with Cross of Lorraine	(a) BM; BN*; MMA (variety undetermined)
				(b) JC; Oxford
				(c) Boston
			13: 5 × 8 grapes with CB + PD countermark	Philadelphia
			nothing, chainlines 29/31mm	BM
W25	*The Virgin and Child with a Rose*	I (with arms)	nothing, chainlines 21/25mm	Boston
		II (arms obliterated)	nothing, chainlines 21/23mm	JC; BN(two); MMA; Boston; Washington
			nothing, chainlines 23/27mm	BM
		III (Le Blond)	nothing, chainlines 33/34mm	JC; Prouté; Boston
		(NB Some of the above impressions have been cut and their states are uncertain; here they have been assigned states on the basis of their paper)		
W26	*Balthasar*	I (pre-Le Blond)	nothing, chainlines 21/22mm	BN; Boston; Amsterdam; Philadelphia
			1: standard grapes	BN
		II (Le Blond)	2: grapes with AB	Copenhagen; Boston
			nothing, chainlines 33/34mm	MMA; Copenhagen
W27	*Caspar*	I (pre-Le Blond)	nothing, chainlines 21/22mm	BN; Amsterdam; Houston
			1: standard grapes	BM; BN; Boston*

Walch No.	Title	State	Watermark	Location
W27	*Caspar*	II (Le Blond)	2: grapes with AB	Copenhagen; MMA; Amsterdam
			nothing, chainlines 33/34mm	Copenhagen; Boston*
W28	*Melchior*	I (pre-Le Blond)	nothing, chainlines 21/22mm	JC; BN; Amsterdam
			1: standard grapes	BN*
		II (Le Blond)	2: grapes with AB	BM; JC; Copenhagen; Boston
			nothing, chainlines 33/34mm	MMA; Copenhagen
W29, 31–45	Uniform sets of Christ and the Apostles		5: small 8 × 5 grapes + AIR countermark	BN
			(five have grapes, six have countermark, five have nothing legible)	
			2: grapes with AB (Le Blond paper)	Copenhagen
			(six have grapes with AB, ten have no watermark)	
W29	*Saint James the Greater*		2: grapes with AB	Amsterdam; Boston*
W31	*Saint Philip*		7: 11 × 7 grapes	Boston*
			nothing, chainlines 33/34mm	Texas
W32	*Saint Bartholomew*		nothing, chainlines 33mm	Boston
W33	*Saint Andrew*		nothing, chainlines 33/34mm	MMA; Boston*
W34	*Saint Thomas*		grapes (uncertain variety), chainlines 34/35mm	Boston
W35	*Saint Thomas*		nothing, chainlines 33/34mm	JC
			grapes (uncertain variety), chainlines 32/25mm	Boston
W36	*Saint James the Greater*		5: small 8 × 5 grapes	Amsterdam; Boston
			6a: AIR countermark, chainlines 33/34mm	JC
			2: grapes with AB	Munich
			nothing, chainlines 33/34mm	BM
W37	*Saint Simon*		5: small 8 × 5 grapes	NYPL*; Boston*
W38	*Saint Jude / Matthias*		nothing, chainlines 26mm	MMA
			6a: AIR countermark, chainlines 33/35mm	JC
			grapes (uncertain variety), chainlines 33/34mm	Boston
W39	*Saint James the Lesser / Jude*		nothing, chainlines 34/36m	MMA; Boston*
W40	*Saint Peter*		5: small 8 × 5 grapes	Boston*
			2: grapes with AB	Boston*
			nothing, chainlines 33/34mm	NYPL
W41	*Saint John*		6a: AIR countermark, chainlines 32/35mm	Boston
			nothing, chainlines 33/34mm	Washington
W42	*Saint Philip*		5: small 8 × 5 grapes	Boston*

Walch No.	Title	State	Watermark	Location
W43	*Saint John*		5: small 8 × 5 grapes	Boston*
W44	*Saint Paul*		nothing, chainlines 22/23mm	Boston
			7: 11 × 7 grapes, chainlines 33/34mm	Boston*
W45	*Christ*		nothing, chainlines 24/25mm	JC
			3: 11 × 6 grapes, chainlines 33/35mm	NYPL*
			6a: AIR countermark, chainlines 33/34mm	Boston (counterproof)
W46	*The Holy Women at the Sepulchre*	I (before signature)	17: crowned H	Boston
			nothing, chainlines 28/30mm	Amsterdam
		II (with signature)	18: H with letters on cross	JC; BM; Boston
			19: posthorn in a shield	MMA; BN*
			13: 5 × 8 grapes with CB + PD countermark	Washington
W47	*The Raising of Lazarus*		8: molecule grapes	Amsterdam; JC; Prouté; Copenhagen; MMA; Boston(three); Philadelphia; Washington
			14: grapes with BV and heart	JC; BN*; Boston*
			15: grapes with COLONBIER in circle	BM
			16: grapes with COLONBIER (variant)	French private coll. (see p.127 under 11)
W (reject)	*The Holy Family with Mary Magdalene and Saint Anne*	I (pre-Le Blond)	1: standard grapes	Amsterdam; BM; JC; BN; Boston
		II (Le Blond)	nothing, chainlines 33/34mm	BN
			nothing, chainlines 29/32mm	Boston

Concordance between Walch and this Catalogue

Walch	Title (as in this catalogue)	Cat. (or Fig.) No.
1	*The Entry of Henri II into Nancy*	1
2	*Ex-Libris of Melchior de la Vallée*	2
3	*The Vision of Saint Norbert in Prémontré*	3
4	*The Virgin Bestowing a Scapular on a Monk*	fig.22 (p.54)
5	*Saint Augustine in Prayer*	fig.23 (p.54)
6	*The Death of Portia*	40
7	*The Virgin and Child with Cradle*	6
8	*The Virgin Wrapping the Child in Swaddling Clothes*	fig.25 (p.60)
9	*The Virgin and Child with Distaff and an Angel*	8
10	*Diana and the Hunter*	38a
11	*Gardener with Urn and Reticule*	35
12	*Gardener with a Basket on her Arm*	33
13	*Gardener with an Ornate Basin*	34
14	*Hortulana*	32
15	*The Holy Family with Saint Catherine, Saint John the Evangelist and an Angel*	5
16	*The Martyrdom of Saint Lucy*	12
17	*Pietà*	15
18	*Hurdy-Gurdy Player Attacking a Pilgrim*	37
19	*Military Figures outside a City*	39
20	*The Adoration of the Magi*	10
21	*Blind Hurdy-Gurdy Player*	36
22	*Three Holy Women*	13
23	*Christ Carrying the Cross*	11
24	*The Annunciation*	9a
25	*The Virgin and Child with a Rose*	7
26	*Balthasar*	29
27	*Caspar*	31a
28	*Melchior*	30a
29	*Saint James the Greater*	21a
30	*Saint Matthew*	fig.30a (p.81)
31	*Saint Philip*	23
32	*Saint Bartholomew*	25a
33	*Saint Andrew*	20
34	*Saint Thomas*	24
35	*Saint Thomas*	24a
36	*Saint James the Greater*	21b
37	*Saint Simon*	28b
38	*Saint Jude/Matthias*	27
39	*Saint James the Lesser/Jude*	26
40	*Saint Peter*	19
41	*Saint John*	22
42	*Saint Philip*	23b
43	*Saint John*	22b
44	*Saint Paul*	17a
45	*Christ*	18
46	*The Holy Women at the Sepulchre*	14
47	*The Raising of Lazarus*	16
reject	*The Holy Family with Mary Magdalene and Saint Anne*	4

Index of Persons and Places